2017

APR 01 2003

D0903134

TIBET

REFLECTIONS FROM THE WHEEL OF LIFE

TIBET

REFLECTIONS FROM THE WHEEL OF LIFE

PHOTOGRAPHS BY THOMAS L. KELLY

TEXT BY CARROLL DUNHAM AND IAN BAKER

FOREWORD BY THE DALAI LAMA

ABBEVILLE PRESS PUBLISHERS

NEW YORK LONDON

For the dakas and dakinis, known and unknown,
who preserve the knowledge of the heart
and keep us dancing on the wheel of life.

In memory of Jeanne Marie Kelly (2/22/22–1/21/93)

JACKET FRONT:
The immensity of the Tibetan landscape
dwarfs a nomad and his flock.

JACKET BACK:
Khampa rider, Paiyul horse festival,
eastern Tibet (see pages 100–101).

FRONTISPIECE:
A monk painting the wheel of life, Dharamsala, India.

Editor: JACQUELINE DECTER

Designer: NAI Y. CHANG

Typography & Cover Design: CHERYL PETERKA

Production Editor: ABIGAIL ASHER

Production Manager: MATTHEW PIMM

Map: OLIVER WILLIAMS

Library of Congress Cataloging-in-Publication Data
Dunham, V. Carroll.
Tibet: reflections from the wheel of life / text by Carroll Dunham and
Ian Baker; photographs by Thomas L. Kelly; foreword by the Dalai Lama.
p. cm.
Includes bibliographical references and index.
ISBN 1-55859-218-0
1. Tibet (China)—Exiles. 2. Refugees, Political—India. 3. Tibet (China)—
Social life and customs. I. Baker, Ian. II. Kelly, Thomas L. III. Title.

DS786.D826 1993
951'.505—dc20
                                                        93-26613
                                                         CIP

ACKNOWLEDGMENTS

Like the wheel of life itself, this book has drawn us ever deeper into the world of love and death, suffering and rejoicing. From marriages and romances to the grievous passing of those dearly loved, we have been guided on our journey by relationships larger than ourselves—opening our eyes to new ways of envisioning the world and its ceaseless changes and disjunctions.

Our greatest thanks must go to our teachers—Chatral Rinpoche, Dudjom Rinpoche, Dilgo Khyentse Rinpoche, Thinley Norbu Rinpoche, Bhakha Tulku, Tulku Orgyen, Chökyi Nyima, Togden Amting, and His Holiness the Dalai Lama—for giving us the confidence to search in the heart of samsara for the treasure of spiritual awakening.

For making this journey of discovery possible among the Tibetan people, our warmest thanks to Sonam Topgyal and Yangkyi Tsering—the light of Tibet House—who taught us our first words of the Tibetan language and introduced us, years ago, to the Tibetans' rich and vibrant culture. Very special thanks are due to Jhampa Wangdu and his wife, Dolkar Lhamo, for their friendship, insight, and assistance over many years. Thanks also to Tashi Tsering, a living Tibetan national treasure, who generously shared his vast scholarship and learning. To Gyurme Wangda—the samurai sage—for his companionship on our first trips into central Tibet, and to Yeshe Choden for invaluable help throughout our journey into Kham. To Kesang Tseten for illuminating discussions on squash courts in Kathmandu, and to his sister Diki for her spontaneity and unique points of view. Special thanks to Trinley Wangmo and Ayang Lhamo—the dakinis of Tashi Jong—for their illuminating perspectives, and to their families for taking us in. To Yönten, Chöden, and Chula—the Goloks of Berkeley and remotest Tibet—for their laughter and boundless charm. And to Saraswati, Soni, and all the other hidden dakinis who usher us into worlds of wonder and delight and keep us spinning on the wheel of life.

Thanks to Ama Topai Adhi and Soepa the ferryman for showing us their grace, courage, and strength after years of suffering under Chinese oppression. And to Doctor Trogawa, Dr. Kunphen, Lhawa Wangchuk, and Tsampa Amchi for revealing how healing concerns more than just the body. To Urgyen and Norbu Tsering and the artists of the Tibetan Institute of Performing Arts for their friendship and patience. And to Lhendrup, Tulku Chime Dorje, Lama Nima, and others we met in Tibet for their rare wisdom and undying spirit. Thanks, too, to the Public Security Bureau officials and undercover police who taught us patience and mindfulness and enriched the intrigue of our travels in eastern Tibet.

Additional gratitude to Hamid Sardar and Frances Harwood for introducing new perspectives at unlikely times and places (lost in impenetrable mists in the hidden land of Kyimolung and dining in piñon groves in northern New Mexico). And not least to our Tibetan family in Nepal—Dawa, Tsering Wangchuk, Zomba, Pema Bhuti, Pasang Thondrup, and Rinchen Norbu—whose wisdom and poise beyond their years make us feel we've been here before and would willingly come back again, to continue a journey with neither beginning nor end. To all the sentient beings—vast as the sky—who share this magician's dream, this ever-spinning wheel of life, thanks!

CONTENTS

FOREWORD

When I meet people in different parts of the world, I am always reminded that as human beings we are all basically alike. The journey from birth to death is something we all share in common, regardless of how differently we choose to live our lives. For Tibetans, this human life is considered a rare and precious opportunity. Buddha said the chance for human life is as rare as a one-eyed turtle surfacing its head through the hole of a single oxen-yoke floating in a vast ocean. From a Buddhist point of view, among the many realms into which we may be born, only as human beings can we develop the qualities of wisdom and compassion that liberate us from deluded existence. To waste even a moment of our precious lives on destructive or self-centered concerns is considered by Tibetans a falling away from our inner-most human nature.

We have all been born on this earth as part of one great human family, and from the very beginning our entire existence has been linked with human love and affection. Birth occurs because of the attraction between a man and a woman. When that passion is refined and made selfless it becomes compassion, such as exists between a mother and her child. From a Buddhist perspective, at one time or another all beings have been our mothers. By reflecting in this way, our selfish and aggressive tendencies will naturally subside, giving birth to our intrinsic Buddha-Nature.

Buddha in Sanskrit means "to be awake," "to be fully conscious." Since beginningless time our intrinsic Buddha-Nature has been obscured by the forces of ignorance, greed, and aggression, as symbolized by the pig, the rooster, and the snake depicted in the center of Tibetan paintings of the Wheel of Life. These negative forces of the mind obscure our limitless inborn potential and are the root cause of our frustrating transmigrations through cyclic existence. By cultivating basic love and kindness, however, we can overcome these inner afflictions and develop happiness and peace not only within ourselves but also among other beings.

The Buddha likened consciousness to an ox cart carving deep grooves in the monsoon mud. By the time of the dry season, or another life, when the same ox cart (or consciousness) comes around again on its accustomed track, its wheels will naturally slip into the ruts it created the previous summer, only this time the ruts have become deeper and more entrenched. Our challenge in each lifetime is to abandon these ruts of narrow-minded habit and, with insight and compassion, forge a new path that leaves no karmic trail. Through developing this innate potential, the wheel of Samsara, or suffering, becomes the wheel of Nirvana, or enlightenment.

But I feel that if day to day you lead a good life, honestly, with love, with compassion, with selflessness, then it will automatically contribute to the attainment of Nirvana. Like the lotus which thrives in mud, the potential for realization grows in the rich soil of our everyday lives. Abstract concepts that are not grounded in this earth, in our own human experience, can never bear fruit.

For more than twelve hundred years the highest ideals of Tibetan civilization have been to emulate the awakened qualities of the Buddha and to strive in freeing all beings from suffering and cyclic existence. To achieve this goal the Tibetan people have evolved a unique and complex culture both earthy and sublime. Although we may not have advanced far technologically, in terms of the development of the mind we are quite rich.

Tibetans are not a politically large and powerful people; we have no great material assets. But our internal resources, found in our way of life, our culture, and our spiritual traditions, have helped us, even in the face of great hardship and suffering, to follow the path of peace and to find comfort in the pursuit of love and compassion. As surely as we are born we will die. But how we choose to live our lives, what seeds of karma we sow through our actions and our thoughts, will determine our state of mind at the moment of death and in the life that follows. If we have lived our lives developing basic human kindness we can be at peace with those around us, and external problems will not trouble us over-much. Then even death, like birth itself, can be welcomed as a rare and precious opportunity to grow beyond our current limitations.

Iconographically, the wheel of life portrays the tendencies and diverse possibilities within samsaric existence. Just as meditating on the wheel of life can help the viewer to see his or her own life with greater clarity, reflecting on the diverse qualities of different cultures can help us to view our own societies from a larger perspective. The present volume introduces Tibetan culture as a journey from life until death—addressing themes that as human beings we all share in common. This book does not present the Tibetan way of life as something to be either embraced or rejected, but offers a way of understanding the Tibetans better as a people.

Looking at the world as others see it and sharing in their thoughts and reflections is itself an act of compassion. Through compassion we develop greater empathy and appreciation for the other beings with whom we share life on this small planet.

By sharing our differing beliefs and unique insights we can enrich each other: not by emulating each other's way of life, but by opening ourselves to other points of view. Within the fascinating range of human cultures and languages, individual likes and dislikes, our basic nature is essentially the same. In our diverse ways we all share the same dreams of achieving happiness and overcoming suffering. It's my sincere hope that the images and voices of the Tibetan people contained in this book may help to spark interest in the Tibetan way of life and the ideals to which it aspires.

HIS HOLINESS TENZIN GYATSO,
THE FOURTEENTH DALAI LAMA OF TIBET

JANUARY 29, 1993

BETWEEN EARTH AND SKY

DANCE OF THE ELEMENTS

In Khawachen—the land of snowy mountains and healing herbs—as Tibetans call their country, the elements are not only primal, they are inescapable. Earth, sky, water, air, and fire are stirred awake by restless, moody winds. Delicate winds have danced across the plateau for centuries, gently brushing Tibetan cheeks and caressing loosely braided hair. Yet these same winds can also stir up vicious blizzards, stinging sandstorms, and raging thunderclouds. On narrow trails hugging precipitous cliffs, winds can sweep whole caravans to their death. Like the people themselves, the winds that encompass them and live within them are both sublime and fierce.

The wind is not alone in its moods. The earth in Khawachen can tremble and split open in an instant. Landslides and avalanches can swallow villages whole. Flash floods can wash away entire hillsides as swollen torrents course violently through precipitous gorges. Scorching geysers can erupt from below the earth's surface, spewing plumes of steaming waters skyward with the wind.

So inescapable are the raw elements of Khawachen that Tibetans believe the elements themselves form the very flesh of their bodies. The outer winds waft incense and bring rustling prayer flags to life, while inner winds, called *lung*, sustain life and sweep through the canyons and channels of Tibetans' bodies from the moment they are conceived until the moment they die. It is the wind, Tibetans believe, that brought forth the beginning of life and earth.

For centuries Tibetans have ascended mountains to offer juniper and other fragrant herbs to mountain and sky deities. Some women, hoping to entice a realized being to enter their womb, burn pots of incense beneath their voluminous dresses. In an old Lhasan folk song an aristocrat, Mrs. Doring, is teased for her incense-blackened rump, caused by her futile attempts to entice the Thirteenth Dalai Lama to reincarnate in her womb. (Photograph by Thomas Laird)

CREATION OF THE EARTH AND PEOPLE

In the thirteenth-century *Chojung* text it is written that long ago, before the existence of time, there was only a dark emptiness of vast space. From this nothingness a soft wind arose, creating an enormous cloud shaped like a thunderbolt. Huge and powerful, this cloud brought forth gushing monsoonlike rains, forming a huge primeval sea. Gentle winds blowing across the surface of the waters caused a light foam that grew thick and heavy. Just as churned milk becomes butter, so earth arose like a great mountain from the churning of wind and water. Seven rings of earth and water encircled the great mountain, home to the gods and surrounded by the continents of the four directions. To the south lay Dzambu Ling, the land of rose apple trees and people.

After the creation of the universe and Dzambu Ling, Tibet still lay submerged beneath the primeval ocean. Indeed, geological records show that twenty million years ago Tibet was covered by the vast Tethys Sea. Through the blessings of Chenresrig, the god of compassion and patron deity of Tibet, the water slowly evaporated, leaving Tibet surrounded by great mountains and peopled by *mimayin*, spirits that can sometimes still be seen.

There were no people in Tibet until the deities Chenresrig and Dolma sent their emanations to a mountain called Konpori in the form of a celibate monkey who lived alone in quiet meditation and a lonely female earth spirit of the rocky crags. The earth spirit sang and cried and begged the monkey to break his vow of celibacy and marry her. The monkey refused until finally, overcome with compassion, he consulted Chenresrig, who told him the time had come for Tibet to have her own children. The monkey and the earth spirit united, and they had six children, one each of the six kinds of creatures that fill the world: gods, demigods, human beings, hungry ghosts, animals, and denizens of hell. Others say the six children represent the six kinds of people found in the different regions of Tibet. As diverse as the tribes and clans of Tibet are, they all seem to share distinctive traits inherited from their mother's untamed spirit and their father's transcendent compassion.

The stories of how the elements formed Tibet and its people are as varied as its landscape and tribes. According to an ancient myth from the early Bon tradition, the pre-Buddhist religion of Tibet, the great god Cha created the universe out of the five elements. He formed heaven with its thirteen ascending layers and earth with its thirteen descending layers. Inside the domes of heaven and earth light and darkness emerged. The coupling of light and darkness created water and sky, whose union produced a son and daughter— the heavenly ancestors of the gods—and the first king, Nyatri Tsangpo, the protector of the Land of Snows.

Anthropologists surmise that the Tibetan people are descended from nomadic Mongolian tribes who migrated south and westward from the central Asian steppes 2,500-3,000 years ago. Over time they settled in the fertile Tsangpo and Yarlung valleys.

Both Bon and Buddhist legends agree that at this time Tibetans felt they needed a king to rule them and their territory. According to Bon legend they sent a message to heaven requesting guidance. They lit juniper incense (*tsang*—the child of father thunder and mother lightning), and a column of smoke, like a ladder, rose in the sky, urging heaven's door to open. From this trap door in the sky, traveling down a luminous column of wind and rainbow light, the sky god reluctantly descended to earth with his son, Nyatri Tsangpo. Tumbling upon the peak of the sacred mountain Yarlha Zampo in central Tibet's Yarlung Valley, the sky god emerged at the center of a mandala:

> *It was the center of the sky,*
> *The middle of the earth and the heart of the country.*
> *An enclosure of glaciers; the head of all rivers.*
> *High mountains, pure earth, an excellent country.*
> *A place where men are born heroes.*
> *Where custom is perfected, where horses grow swift.*

Tibet cultivated a breed of "divinely mad" Tantric specialists to subdue the unruly spirits of the earth, water, and sky. Deep in trance, this Bonpo lama uses a variety of ritual instruments for the task. In his right hand he holds a drum, chopper, and the hair of a hundred dead and living people; in his left, a thigh-bone trumpet, dagger, and bell. He is also said to carry blood from a black ass, earth from a black stupa, and black soil from the place where dead bodies are flayed and fed to the vultures.

The first seven kings lived on earth by day and ascended from their mountain abodes to heaven at night. In this way their mountain homes became sacred places of worship—ladders to the sky. Winding processions of pilgrims can still be found ascending mountains to coax the local deity to descend from the sky down a ladder of curling juniper smoke.

When Buddhism came to Tibet, some of the mountains became Buddhist, too. The three hills of Lhasa—Chakpori, Pongwari, and

Marpori—are the soul mountains of the Buddhist deities Vajrapani, Manjushri, and Chenresrig. Some mountains are benevolent and some are fierce, protective warriors. King of all mountains, Mount Kailas, or Kang Rinpoche (Jewel of the Snows), in far western Tibet is viewed as the navel of the world, the physical point where the heavens unite with earth. For more than two thousand years pilgrims have been drawn to this remote mountain, which followers of Bon worship as the place where the great saint Shenrab descended to earth from the sky. In traditional Buddhist cosmology Kang Rinpoche is linked to Mount Meru, the great mythological mountain at the center of the universe.

Many mountains in Tibet are wedded to lakes, thereby uniting sky, earth, and the underworld. Kang Rinpoche, for example, is wedded to Mapham Yumtso, or Lake Manasarovar, and Nyenchen Tanglha to Lake Namtso in northern Tibet. Reflecting wisdom, sacred lakes reveal hidden portents to those who gaze into them with faith and devotion. But lakes can contain more than prophetic visions.

"*Namtso* means 'sky lake,' " Lhendrop, an old nomad, told us as he spun wool beside a teapot that was warming in a pile of glowing yak-dung embers. "At morning sunrise you can see Guru Rinpoche's handprint white on the sea, and in the evening the mountain's shadow makes the handprint dark. In the old days yogis meditating beside the lake used to see seahorses, seasheep, and seayak who lived at the bottom of the lake. They didn't have any hair, and they'd wander up on shore grazing from time to time. But we haven't seen any in a long time. The Chinese want to develop a fishing industry here, but the old people think if they fish they'll disturb the deities. If the deities become angry there will be more snow in winter and the animals will give birth to deformed offspring."

GEOLOGICAL DRAMA

One has only to consider the forces at work in the geological creation of Tibet's formidable mountains and lakes to understand their deification. Some forty-five million years ago, in one of the most dramatic geological events in the formation of the earth's crust, the Indian subcontinent collided with the Asian land mass, thrusting it upward to create the Himalayan range and the vast central Asian plateau. The size of western Europe, stretching 1,200

miles wide and 750 miles long, the Tibetan plateau is surrounded by the earth's highest mountains—the Himalayas to the south, the Karakorum, Kunlun, Min Shan, and Ta-hsueh Shan to the west, north, and east.

THE BODY OF THE LAND

To Tibetans, the entire geography of the country is a sacred realm where mountains are thought of as pillars that hold up the vault of the sky like tent poles or, alternatively, anchor it to the earth like the pegs of a nomad's tent. In the tenth-century text *Mani Kabum*, the terrain of Tibet is described as the body of a supine demoness. The seventh-century Chinese princess Wen Chen Konjo, wife of Tibetan king Srongsten Gampo, is credited with this discovery. She had been having difficulty transporting a statue of Buddha across the country, so she consulted her geomantic charts and "understood that this snow land country as a whole is like a demoness lying on her back." To render her harmless, Buddhist *chortens* and "earth-subduing" temples were built on precise points in the landscape of the demoness's body. The Jokhang—Tibet's most revered temple, located in the center of Lhasa—strikes the demoness's heart like a *purbu*, the shaman's ritual dagger, immobilizing her and preventing her from causing any harm.

Since the flesh of the land was perceived as alive with spirit, the first twenty-seven kings of Tibet ruled the country with the help of exorcists, shamans, and priests who worked to maintain harmony with the multitude of local earth spirits inhabiting the water, rocks, and trees. Dwelling in obscure recesses of the country, these spirits were capable of unleashing earthquakes, floods, and other natural disasters if not properly appeased. Serpentlike water spirits, or *lu*, lived at the bottom of lakes, guarding secret treasures. The sacred juniper tree, a popular abode of certain spirits, figures prominently in Bon ritual practice. Its branches are offered in sacrifices, and its berries are used as a narcotic to induce ecstatic trances.

We once visited an *amchi*—an herbal doctor—who lives near a Tibetan refugee camp in Nepal's Thak Khola Valley. We trudged up to the summit of a flat-topped mountain geomantically considered the center of a mandala—a sacred spot encircled in the four directions by looming snow-laden Himalayan peaks. An ancient juniper tree rose starkly out of the barren soil near the mountain's summit.

"This is where the *dakinis* meet and dance," Tsampa Amchi solemnly whispered to us, referring to invisible female deities who inhabit the air.

The Thak Khola winds howl and blow, penetrating deep into our bones. Pema Dolkar, a resident of the Tsedruk refugee camp, says the wind's fury must be caused by the cantankerous ogress with sagging breasts who lives in the canyon and who was tamed by Padmasambhava, Tibet's great yogin saint who conquered local demons and ogresses and converted them into Buddhist protector deities. Tsampa Amchi disagrees with Pema's interpretation, saying that Padmasambhava was meditating here and he felt hot so he blew—Phat!—and that is why the wind blows so relentlessly. "This is the breath of Padmasambhava," he says. "This wind is healing. If skinny people eat the pure air of these mountains, they will grow healthy and fat."

Later, thunder roars and lightning flashes. "The dragons are roaring," Tsampa Amchi says simply as we make our way to his home in the descending dark. "Sometimes you can see their tails slipping into the clouds surrounding the mountains."

The Tibetan landscape is alive with reminders of its people's reverence toward the invisible realms. On steep mountain passes cairns of stones are offered in reverence to local divinities and protector gods. Cloth flags stamped with Buddhist prayers are strung up in high, windy places or near rivers so that the wind and water may transmit the wisdom of the prayers to all sentient creatures. We once came across a simple monk murmuring chants as he stamped the rushing stream beside him with a woodblock of prayers.

THE FOUR DIRECTIONS

Like Europeans before Copernicus who saw the earth as the center of the universe, Tibetans saw themselves as the center of a cosmic and terrestrial mandala—a sacred circular diagram with four cardinal directions. To the east lay China, the land of divination and calculation; to the south lay India, the land of religion; to the west lay Persia and Byzantium, lands of jewels, wealth, and profitable trade; and in the north lived Turks and Uighurs in the land of horses, weapons, and war. The Yarlung Valley, where the first king descended from the sky, was the mandala's center, surrounded by magical animals protecting each of the directions: the white snow lioness ruled in the east; the blue dragon in the south; the tiger in the west; and the wild yak in the north.

Spiritually, Tibet was also envisioned as a mandala, a sacred realm with the Yarlung Valley kings at the center until Srongsten Gampo moved the capital to Lhasa in the seventh century. Later the Dalai Lamas residing in the Potala Palace became the divine ruling center. With entrances into Lhasa from the east, west, north, and south, each direction of the country is known for its distinctive qualities. As Wen Chen Konjo remarked from Lhasa,

The eastern mountains are like heaps of flowers
The southern mountains are like glittering jewels
The western mountains are like stacks of stupas
The northern mountains are like snow-white conch shells

In all directions of this sacred and diverse landscape, Tibet is alive with mountain deities, sky goddesses, visionary lakes, and serpentine beings of the underworld. Tibetans do not seek to conquer the elements, but rather to harmonize with their inescapable presence. Worshiping the spirits of the wind, sky, water, rocks, and mountains, Tibetans embrace the elements of which they themselves are composed and which reside as deities within their bodies. With every breath, Tibetans inhale the cold, thin air mingled with particles of water and earth, circulating life-bestowing essences throughout the inner landscape of the body. As the inner winds cease to blow, the fire in the belly becomes but an ember, the earth element of the flesh and the water element of the blood begin to erode and evaporate like a parched riverbed, and the body is returned to the elements: thrown in a river for the fish to feed on, buried in the earth for the worms to eat, extinguished in a blaze of fire, or placed on a mountaintop and offered to the birds and sky.

According to Bon myth, the first Tibetans descended from the sky to the mountaintops on magical ladders of rainbow light. (Photograph by Ian Baker)

This center of heaven
This core of the earth
This heart of the world,
Fenced round by snow,
The headland of all rivers,
Where the mountains are high and
The Land is pure.

—The Dunhuang Documents,
  eighth and ninth centuries

Sunlight penetrating through dark clouds illumines a herd of sheep grazing on the vast Tingri plains of south-central Tibet. Bon legend interprets clouds as the wool of grazing celestial sheep. Sometimes the celestial sheep scratch heaven's surface, causing turquoise stones to tumble from the sky.

The rolling grasslands of eastern Tibet stretch behind a horseman on a rearing white stallion. White horses have great symbolic connotations in Tibet. Legend has it that Shenrab, the founder of the pre-Buddhist Bon religion, was led into Tibet by his magical white horse. As a result, horses are known as carriers of the religion and figure prominently on prayer flags, called *lungta,* or "windhorses." In Tibetan Buddhist scriptures the mind is often likened to a wild horse that if kept untrained is of limited use.

A Bonpo lama at the entrance to a cave used for dark retreat in Lubrak, Nepal. Retreatants traditionally withdraw into the complete darkness of such caves for as long as three years, three months, and three days in search of the luminous light residing within and around them. Incense is sent billowing skyward to please the deities and beckon them to descend to earth.

At Tashitoh in northern Tibet, the rock formations have rich mythological and mystical associations for Buddhists. "The Chinese destroyed our statues and paintings, but they can't tear down our praying rocks, now can they?"

—LHENDROP, last living survivor of a Chinese massacre of monks at Tashitoh Monastery, Lake Namtso, Tibet.

Tibetans believe human beings are composed of the elements: earth, wind, fire, water, and air. When enlightened beings die, their bodies are said to dissolve into rainbow light.

Considered the navel of the universe, where heaven and earth embrace, Mount Kailas, or Kang Rinpoche, whose name means "jewel of the snows," has attracted devout pilgrims to its base for more than two thousand years. In the thirteenth century the Buddhist yogin Milarepa and the Bon shaman Naro Bonchung competed in duels of magic for possession of Mount Kailas's coveted summit. Milarepa's followers were disconcerted to see Naro Bonchung flying to the summit astride his shaman drum, while Milarepa remained deep in meditation. But at the last moment Milarepa soared past Naro Bonchung, winning the mountain for Buddhism. The vertical gash on the south face of the sacred mountain is said to have been gouged out by Naro Bonchung's drum, which he dropped in alarm at seeing the yogin overtake him.

Mapham Yumtso in western Tibet is revered by Hindus as Lake Manasarovar. Gandhi requested that his ashes be scattered beside this sacred lake, and Nehru's one last regret was not having seen its turquoise waters. According to Buddhist mythology, the Buddha's mother bathed in the lake before giving birth to him. Local legend tells of a great saint who wanted to win the hand of a fair princess but first had to pass a series of trials, including killing a wild yak. The saint tried to drown the beast in the lake, but only its body remained submerged, giving the lake its name—Lake of the Invincible Consort.

OPPOSITE
Padma Sambhava, painting, fourteenth century. Myth and history blur in the tales of the great Padmasambhava, Tibet's most beloved saint, who tamed demons, converted many barbaric kingdoms to Buddhism, and achieved extraordinary longevity. Here he is attended by his two consorts, Bengali princess Madarava, on his right, and Yeshe Tsogyal, Tibetan queen turned yogini, on his left.

Temples and monasteries of Lhasa, painted in eastern Tibet in the first half of the nineteenth century. In the seventh century Tibetan king Srongsten Gampo moved the capital from the Yarlun Valley to Lhasa. Here Lhasa is depicted as a vision of a pure land, which is how Tibetans perceive the city. The Potala Palace, residence of the Dalai Lamas, is in the center; surrounding it are the three main monasteries of the Gelugpa order: Drepung, Sera, and Ganden. In the lower right-hand corner is the Jokhang, the most sacred temple of Tibet and the oldest, dating to about A.D. 640.

CHILDHOOD

BECOMING

IN SEARCH OF A WOMB

Withdrawing the smoldering juniper branch from the flames, Tashi lifts the tent flap and carries the smoking branch out into the darkness. Gingerly raising the folds of her woolen gown, she holds the branch beneath her, letting the fragrant juniper smoke curl between her thighs, cleansing and sanctifying her womb door. A revered lama has died in the last month, and Tashi is eager to entice this great consciousness into her womb with the aroma of juniper.

Returning to the tent, she loosens her *chuba* (dress), and joins her sleeping husband, Dawa, in the folds of sheepskins and Chinese comforters that make their bed. Tonight they are alone. Dawa's parents and younger brother and sister have gone with the herd to the summer grazing pastures. Tashi's skin and long braids glisten with yak butter as she lays her head beside her husband's. Shadows from the hearth's last flames dance on the sloping walls of their yak-hair tent. Under the blankets, Dawa reaches over and pulls Tashi toward him.

Meanwhile, high up in the sky, a restless *namshe*—a disembodied consciousness and seeker of existence—roams the earth in search of a womb. With his golden "enjoyment body" the size of a five-year-old's, he flies uncontrollably through solid mountains and thickets of trees, careening beneath fences, driven by the karmic winds of desire and attachment. He passes over his own rotting corpse, anguished at the vision of his own death.

Pema Chunzum, born February 14, in the year of the earth monkey, Kathmandu, Nepal.

Today I was born into the family of Buddhas;
A child of the Buddhas I've become today.
　　　　　　　　　　　　　—SANTIDEVA

MEMORIES OF DYING

Plagued by incessant, terrifying hallucinations, his emotions veer from joy to sorrow, sorrow to despair. Like a child abandoned by its mother or a fish thrown flapping onto hot sand, the namshe is haunted by his death, when the elements that composed his body collapsed. The earth winds rose and he felt he was suffocating under a huge landslide until the water winds blew and, desperately gasping for air, he was swept away in a swollen river until the fire winds rose and he felt himself being consumed in the flames of a blazing forest fire only to be carried off by gusting winds. The horrifying memories propel him onward. He has to get out of here. He must find a body.

He has been in the *bardo*, the state between death and rebirth, for almost forty-two days. He has only seven more days to find a womb. All he can remember of the death that brought him to the bardo is the terrible confusion, the misery, and the pain. But the clear, luminous light—that piercing, beginningless light like an immaculate dawn sky cleansed by autumn rains, like a blazing sun reflected in a mirror, that sheer, intense, luminous yet annihilating, light—he remembers the fear of it extinguishing him. And yet that vision recedes into unconscious darkness, utter pervasive black.

Soon the darkness dissolves into a glowing orange-red sunset, each ray a dancing deity of rainbow light. "Where do all these deities and lights come from?" he wonders as the images flicker and dissolve in a piercing flash of lightning more brilliant than a hundred thousand suns. Suddenly, thunder, like a furious dragon, roars with a ferocity greater than a hundred thousand thunderclaps, shaking the very core of his being.

Dazed, enveloped in mist, he drifts into the pale Land of the Dead. Yama, the Lord of Death, appears holding a mirror. Peering into the mirror, the namshe sees the reflection of all his past actions, good and bad. Separating the virtuous and nonvirtuous actions of his past life into piles of black and white pebbles, Yama decides the namshe's karmic fate: the realm—deity, demon, or human—into which he will be reborn. Suddenly a host of terrifying Heruka deities appear to leap out and, with blood dripping from their fangs, dance luridly on his corpse. He panics and faints, only to find himself surrounded by a rainbow of light as dazzling as a parasol of peacock feathers.

In the far distance he thinks he sees a lake adorned with male and female swans. Is this a sign he will be reborn as a human? Before he can ponder this, he finds himself in the midst of a crowded bazaar. The pleasing fragrance of juniper pervades his senses. Gazing downward, he sees a tent on the Tibetan plateau.

ENTERING THE WOMB DOOR

Espying the shadows of a couple making love, he is filled with desire and envy and swoops down from the sky into the tent to join them. The sight of his father repels him and although without a body and without form he turns to embrace his mother. The force of Tashi and Dawa's mounting passion causes a self-effacing bliss to spread throughout their cells and along the 144,000 neural channels within their united bodies.

Suddenly the namshe can see nothing more than Tashi's pulsating lotus gate. At the same moment Dawa—overcome with desire—opens Tashi's womb door with a warm flood of semen. Desperately seeking entrance, the namshe soars into his mother's womb. Hearing peaceful and pleasant sounds, he feels he's entering an opulent palace that will be his home, a place of rest after so much wandering. But his substanceless karmic body is instantly enclosed in blood and vital fluids, which rapidly begin to form the embryo of a human body around him.

After making love, Tashi rolls over. Her body relaxed, her mind spacious. The pleasure she and her husband experienced was more intense than either had ever experienced before. Could she have conceived? Her aunt once told her that bliss is much stronger when conception occurs. Falling stars shoot through the summer sky around the tent, and Dawa begins to snore. Tashi's mind wanders toward the goats that need milking in the morning. "Will I dream of fruit or conch shells or turquoise or gold or sunbeams?" she wonders, all signs that a namshe has nested in her womb. She sighs, chants a few mantras, and drifts off to sleep.

THE ELEMENTS FORM A BODY

Meanwhile, inside her womb, forces are busily at work. The namshe's life force soars like a bird in the sky inscribing invisible magical signs. Tracing the Tibetan letter AH!, the first sound and letter of existence, the vital force churns Dawa's sperm with the inner elements and winds of Tashi's ovum to create an embryo as viscous as yogurt and as circular as a small egg. During the first month the inner winds form a body as solid as cheese and resembling a minnow. By the seventh week, the embryo is as firm as a piece of wood and looks like a turtle; its central channel begins to grow upward from its navel like a tree, creating centers of neural energy called chakras at the heart, throat, and top of the head before shooting roots downward to create the lower chakras. Growing and changing with each month, the fetus goes from looking like a frog to a wild boar to a lion to a dwarf, and by the sixth month he resembles a shiny pink piglet.

A wind called remembrance of previous lives gently stirs during the twenty-fourth week in the womb, and the unborn child's awareness becomes very clear and he sees his former lives; he sees his past births, his past mothers, and realizes he was no one special, just an ordinary being with a continuous pattern of human faults. He has spun round on this wheel of life countless times, and yet he still has not learned that the primordial nature of his mind is luminous, unobstructed Clear Light. Until that recognition dawns, he will not be free from the recurring cycles of sorrow, frustration, and discontent.

Tashi's belly is round and plump beneath her chuba as she continues her daily routine. Awakening one morning, she remembers her dream of a turquoise-studded conch shell and herds of wild stallions surrounded by rays of light, and she smiles, knowing that her pregnancy is proceeding safely. Her mother-in-law, Dolma, notices that Tashi's right hip is raised, that she sways to the right when she walks, and that her navel is high. "Your baby is a boy," she pronounces matter-of-factly, and turns to resume milking the sheep.

Because his mother's passion during love making was stronger than his father's, this being becomes a boy, not a girl, and he curls up comfortably on the right side of his mother's belly. Gradually he comes to dislike his womb home and by the thirty-sixth week yearns to leave. "It's so cramped in here," he thinks, "so smelly and dark. I feel imprisoned." Flailing his arms and kicking his feet in discontent, he tries to let Tashi know he wants to leave the womb he once so desperately sought. The winds in his body turn him upside down, and with his hands drawn back like a flying superhero, head first, feet up, the primal causal-energy wind thrusts him from his mother's womb, through the door of the uterus, out the lotus gate, and into the wide world.

Emanations of Emptiness—Deities of the Bardo, thangka painting. Following the fleeting appearance of the clear light of death, ordinary beings enter into bardo, a hallucinatory interim state between this life and the next. Those trained in the esoteric path of the inner T0antras learn to recognize the intrinsic nature of mind in the form of colors, lights, and peaceful and wrathful deities emanating from mandala spheres within the decomposing body.

A young Buddhist monk, Jokhang Temple, Lhasa. Religious practice is integrated into Buddhists' lives from an early age.

GROWING UP

PASTIMES

As babies grow into children, uttering noises that soon become words, toddling beyond the reassuring folds of their mothers' skirts, they develop awareness of the mystery of the surrounding world—a world ripe for exploration and discovery. Through ignorance and lack of experience children begin learning the lessons of life: the searing burn of scorching coals; the buck of a wild stallion; the bite of a vicious mastiff. Yet Tibetans recognize that not all children are newcomers on the merry-go-round of existence. Though their bodies may be very young, their insight and experience may be far greater than their years.

The first Tibetan children I ever lived with were young nuns in a Kathmandu nunnery. Children first, aspiring Buddhist practitioners second, they were irrepressibly naughty, rambunctious, high-spirited little girls with radiant personalities, spontaneous grace, and an inherent sense of reverence for the world around them. Their exuberance and vitality were in no way tempered by the requisite burgundy robes and shaved heads.

I was struck by the strict protocol and rigorous discipline that governed their young lives. They rose each morning at four A.M. to light incense and chant the ancient liturgy invoking Tara—the Bodhisattva goddess who grants liberation. During the day they memorized sacred texts and performed various chores, such as polishing butter lamps and sorting laundry, until it was time to unfold their bedrolls and murmur their bedtime prayers. I never ceased to marvel at their tireless energy, though on occasion I would catch a young nun yawning and dozing off during evening prayers, for which she would incur a resounding thwack from an older nun as a reminder that to be born Buddhist means striving always to be fully awake.

Although these girls were strong individuals, I came to be most impressed with their cultivated awareness of others. Many were scrappy and selfish, but they were taught empathy for all sentient creatures. Out of habit, the little nuns would delicately sweep the bugs out of the kitchen rather than smash them back into the cycle of suffering and involuntary rebirth.

While a child of Tibetan refugees in Switzerland may watch Teenage Mutant Ninja Turtle movies on videocassette, his cousin in Tibet might be fashioning a slingshot from yak hair or making garlands out of meadow flowers. When not immersed in chores or school, clusters of kids can be found shooting marbles, hopping squares of hopscotch scrawled in the dust, or practicing feats of archery. Some children play a game called *gitee*, which involves hitting a stone with a small coin, while others kick balls of vulture features aloft in a Tibetan form of hacky sack called *chibi*. Gampo Tashi, leader of the Tibetan resistance movement, loved to wrestle and climb rocks as a child. The Dalai Lama used to enjoy hiding out in hen coops with the chickens, and when he was older he'd skate with glee across the polished floors of the Potala Palace.

The Dalai Lama's mischievous older brother Thupten Jigme Norbu discovered that sometimes the curiosity of childhood exploration could lead to disaster, such as the time he snuck into the altar room to try to roast a potato over a flickering butter lamp. Unfortunately, the potato fell over, causing melted butter to spill out of the lamp and the statue behind it to burst into flames. "I ran from the room screaming in horror, only to meet the wrath of my mother."

More frightening than parental wrath was the unknown. The Dalai Lama used to be terrified of crawling into bed in his dark, vermin-infested room in the Potala. An ancient fresco in the Jokhang, Lhasa's central shrine, depicts owls that snatch small boys after dark, and the Dalai Lama was petrified that an owl would come and abduct him from his lonely room.

Bedtime tales about the great hero Gesar of the kingdom of Ling, who waged victorious battles with neighboring tribes, rescued and seduced fair damsels in distress, rode flying stallions, and wielded magical swords that sang warnings when the enemy was near, helped keep fears of the dark far away.

HARDSHIP

The most difficult aspect of childhood for Tempa Choepel, who grew up in Tibet during the Chinese Cultural Revolution, was enduring *thamzing* (class-struggle sessions), in which his father was publicly ridiculed and severely beaten. "The head of the working committee would exhort us children to stand up and speak out against our parents. He said they belonged to the old system, were rotten and would soon die anyway, but that we children were only 1 percent rotten and 99 percent good and that a bright future awaited us as members of the glorious communist state. After the meetings my mother and I would have to help my father hobble back to our room. I would bury my head in the bed weeping while mother wiped the blood off his bruised face."

For Sonam Topgyal, whose mother died during the exodus from Tibet in 1959 and whose father was compelled to work on Indian road crews, childhood was not always a pleasant time. "I was placed in an orphanage. There wasn't much money so they put sand into the dumpling dough. We used to get one pair of shoes a year. Once I took mine off when I went to play in a huge pile of sand. I jumped into the pile and when I came back, my shoes were gone. I was forced to wear plastic bags wrapped around my feet through that whole winter." Sonam found solace not only with his friends but also in his studies. A poor nomad from the Kyirong region, in exile Sonam had the opportunity for an education he never would have received in Tibet before the Chinese came or even now under Chinese rule.

SCHOOLING

There is a Tibetan saying that "knowledge must be burned, hammered, and beaten like pure gold before one can wear it as an ornament." Discipline in Tibetan schools is traditionally very harsh. As the Tibetan scholar Lobsang Lhalungpa points out, for Tibetans "the object of education is to crack the shell of ignorance, expand the intellect, and thereby encourage the achievement of supreme wisdom, the essence of enlightenment." Tibetans believe that their need for knowledge—the lessons they must learn through daily human life—brought them into the cycle of existence in the first place. As a result, education is highly revered, valued, and encouraged.

Lobsang Nyima, headmaster of the Atisha primary school in Jawalekel, Nepal, impresses upon his students the need for education. "It is important to study hard, even if you are to die the very next day. Because education is the one thing that nothing, not even death, can take away," he tells them. "Those subjects learned in previous incarnations will come more easily in this lifetime because they don't have to be learned all over again—you must simply refresh your memory. Slower students are simply seeing the material for the first time. To offset the lack of learning in past lives and ensure success in future lives, it is critical to work diligently and relentlessly now, everyday; you must not waste a minute."

TULKUS

Cymbals and horns clamor in anticipation from the direction of Dilgo Khyentse's monastery behind the Boudhanath stupa in Nepal's Kathmandu Valley. The ornate monastery, rich with intricate Bhutanese murals and dangling crystal chandeliers, is crammed with hundreds of lay people clutching blessing scarves and envelopes full of money offerings. They have all come to be blessed by Pema Wangchen, an eight-year-old child whom Dilgo Khyentse Rinpoche, an immense lama of extraordinary presence, is enthroning as a *tulku*—a lama of high attainment who is recognized as the reincarnation of his predecessor. Eyes barely blinking, the young boy's head meets the eighty-five-year-old master's forehead. Khyentse Rinpoche bestows his own realized qualities on the child and perceives that with training, this child's

The tulku of Dzangar Monastery rides inside a horse-drawn palanquin at the foot of the Kemar Pass, Gansu, eastern Tibet.

Lu Zo, youngest son of the ruler of Yongning, flanked by his brother and sister. Authorities in Lhasa declared Lu Zo to be the incarnation of a high lama of the Drepung Monastery.

mindstream will become fully enlightened. The young boy is ripe with latent wisdom and all-penetrating compassion.

Two weeks later, we make our way to Pema Wangchen's hillside monastery to meet this revered child and his parents. Scrambling up the monastery's steep steps, we are met by Pema Wangchen's father, Ralo Rinpoche, and his consort—Pema Wangchen's mother. The little tulku screams and charges past us, waving his toy sword like a wrathful incarnation of the Bodhisattva Manjushri, the sword-wielding slayer of ignorance. With a sprightly yell, he leaps up and dashes out the door with a young monk attendant scampering behind him. He then scurries back to the reassuring folds of his mother's chuba. Hugging her knees, he shyly turns around and gives us a radiant smile. His father tells us: "Two disciples saw dragons dancing in the sky the day he was born. After his birth, Pema didn't close his eyes for two days. He stayed awake and never cried. Chatral Rinpoche was invited to bless the child. He said, 'This child is a tulku. This is Chupo Padam. He has been reborn many times.'"

Sweet-smelling incense rises from the juniper boughs burning on a coal brazier. Ralo Rinpoche explains to us how a realized consciousness chooses its birth, unlike the rest of us, who are thrown back into the wheel of life by the forces of greed, lust, and anger. "Ordinary people's rebirth is determined by their past actions but a tulku chooses the womb of his birth."

A rattle is thrown down the stairs—thump, thump, bang—after which a delighted child's peals of laughter fill the air. "What are your hopes for him?" we ask his mother.

"I only hope he will give others much happiness," she says.

KHAMTRUL RINPOCHE

The Tibetan refugee camp of Tashi Jong is nestled into the rolling hills of Himachal Pradesh in northwestern India. At this refugee camp another young incarnate lama, Khamtrul Rinpoche, lives with his teacher, Togden Achu. On the way up the steep, winding trail to his quarters we are soaked by monsoon rains, but at last we find refuge inside the young tulku's dimly lit room. We prostrate ourselves before a slightly built, almost feline-looking boy curled up in his robes behind a low table covered with Buddhist scriptures. A soft, crescent-moon smile spreads across his porcelain-fine face when he sees us. Togden Achu, a sinuous yogin with thick matted dreadlocks, stands beside him, gently tolerating the intrusion into the boy's study time. The teacher's title, *togden*, which means "realized being," indicates that young Khamtrul's upbringing is far from normal. Reputedly one of the last living yogins possessing *siddhi* (magical) powers—the result of his intense Tantric practices, Togden Achu is said to have saved the last villagers of Khampagar in Tibet, who huddled near him while an entire Chinese squadron fired bullets at him, which he brushed away like so many disturbing gnats.

Light filters into the dark room onto the vast pile of Buddhist texts that Khamtrul is studying. Not a moment of his childhood is wasted, as his teachers constantly challenge him to recall all his knowledge from former lives. Villagers come in and with humility bow and prostrate themselves before the shy child, who blesses them by laying his hand on their heads, as he has done on ours. Could he be a realized being? An old woman who has traveled far to see Khamtrul Rinpoche in his young new body is so overwhelmed by the boy's soft, sweet smile and gentle eyes, which transcend time, space and death, that she weeps with joy. For her, there is no doubt.

A playful tulku breaks protocol during a ceremonial procession of monks at Kathok Monastery in eastern Tibet, once famous for its highly accomplished yogins, many of whom attained the ability to levitate and fly.

Nomad children peering through the opening of their tent, Changtang, Tibet.

A small child at play in the fields near Lake Namtso, northern Tibet.

Ani Tenzin with two young disciples, Swayambhu, Kathmandu Valley, Nepal. "The Chinese teach children to believe in only what they see," she says. "We teach our young nuns that there is more to life than what the eyes can see."

Chokyi Wangmo, a young Buddhist
nun who recently arrived in Nepal
from Tibet, eyes the camera with
a mixture of curiosity and shyness that
belies her usually mischievous nature.

A novice monk peers out from behind the curtains of a monastery, Shigatse, Tibet.

Schoolchildren at the Tibetan Children's Village, Darjeeling, India.
"A Tibetan who doesn't know the Tibetan language is like a bird with
only one wing."

—KARMA, SNOW LION FOUNDATION

Young monks chanting scripture, Mahabuddha Vihara Monastery, Clementown, India. "Education is to crack the shell of ignorance, expand the intellect, and thereby encourage the achievement of supreme wisdom, the essence of enlightenment."
—LOBSANG LHALUNGPA, TIBETAN SCHOLAR

Young Tibetan refugee boys dancing to the Hindi hit song "I am a disco—disco dancer!" at a wedding, Tashi Jong refugee camp, India.

Passing bicyclists take no notice as unclad street children, fresh from a dip in the river, sing for alms on a Lhasa street.

ADOLESCENCE

COMING OF AGE

Ripening

A young boy's voice deepens. Breasts emerge on a girl's chest, and the telltale blood of her grandmothers marks her transition to womanhood. Our bodies tell us there is no going back to childhood. At no time in our lives does the disturbing question "Who am I and where am I going?" present itself more insistently than in adolescence. Some Tibetan teenagers opt to become monks or nuns; others venture into business, court lovers, and eventually marry.

For many Tibetan youths, the search for identity involves flirting with pop culture. In India and Nepal, teenagers may have posters of Sumar Khan, Kunda Dixit, or Sri Devi—popular Hindi movie stars—as well as images of Tom Cruise, Michael Jackson, Brooke Shields, or Phoebe Cates plastered on their bedroom walls. In contrast, their city cousins in Tibet may adorn their walls with pictures of Ellen Chan, Maggie Cheung, and Ronnee Yip—the latest sex symbols from Guangzhaou, China.

Tashi Kelsang, a flamboyant twenty-two-year-old performer at the Tibetan Institute of Performing Arts in Dharamsala, India, enjoys singing in Tibetan operas and proudly identifies with his cultural heritage. Yet, he complains: "The elders won't let us play rock 'n' roll. They say we should play only traditional songs. But we are young, why should we be so limited? Our biggest aim is to be modern.

"I've seen video cassettes of the Tibetan operas performed in Tibet for Chinese propaganda. In many ways, their performances are much better than ours. They have a modern stage, beautiful costumes, and the singing is excellent. I appreciate their skills. But their

Khampa teenagers from Minyag, eastern Tibet.

operas are artificial—not from the heart. We need to perform these more than they do. We perform them because we want our culture to survive."

To my question concerning youth in exile, Aten, a seventy-year-old Khampa from eastern Tibet who fought valiantly for Tibet's freedom, responded, "Their biggest struggle is for freedom. In every Tibetan's heart this is the struggle. I can't guarantee that all Tibetans will return if Tibet gets its freedom, but I am sure that most of them will."

The Tibetan Youth Congress in India is one of the last flames of "radical" ferment left in exile today. Lhasang Tsering, the former head of the turbulent Youth Congress, is one of the few Tibetans who openly buck the Dalai Lama's line of nonviolence. He believes the only way Tibetans can regain Tibet from Chinese rule is through military struggle. "What has nonviolence achieved for us in the past forty years? We are no closer to a free Tibet than we were forty years ago. Time is running out."

In exile, demonstrations have become annual rituals for rallying the community and reminding them of their Tibetan identity and the plight of their homeland. With an enemy as formidable as the People's Republic of China, faith and conviction must combat hopelessness and frustration. A handful of committed Tibetan teenagers continue to stage hunger strikes, protests, and demonstrations. "We cannot give up hope," Tashi Kelsang reminds me. "Without hope, we have nothing."

Not all young Tibetans dream of a Tibet free from Chinese rule, however. Nineteen-year-old Tseten Dolkar from Lhasa is in India studying English but plans to return to Tibet. "In Tibet I never knew there was such a thing as a Tibetan flag. I never knew about the freedom movement. When I first came to India I remember seeing the March 10 demonstrations protesting the Chinese occupation of Tibet and wondering, 'Why are they shouting?'"

Twenty-year-old Ngawang Tsepak knows why they are shouting. On September 2, 1989, she and eight other nuns staged a demonstration for Tibetan independence, for the return of the Dalai Lama, and for freedom of religion. The demonstration took place in Lhasa during a Chinese performance of a Tibetan opera. After being arrested and handcuffed, Ngawang Tsepak was driven to Gutsa prison and stripped naked. In the prison courtyard her hands were tied behind her back and she was suspended by her arms from a tree in a torture position Tibetans call the "airplane." She was then given electric shocks to make her confess or reveal other names. When she was finally taken down, both her shoulders were dislocated. She escaped to India in 1991. Her head freshly shorn, Ngawang Tsepak once again lives the life of a nun, but now in a country not her own. She lights butter lamps and circumambulates the Dalai Lama's residence each day, the breath of prayers for her fellow inmates at Gutsa prison fresh on her lips.

ROMANCE

From the heart within my breast
I can think of only one thing,
that is you, who have stolen my heart.
—Khampa love song, eastern Tibet

As the body ripens, so too does the heart. Many Tibetan sages warn that romantic love is not without its dangers. Chökyi Nyima Rinpoche, a lama in Kathmandu, likens falling in love to "licking honey off a razor." Arousing passions and emotional attachments, love can lead to both ecstasy and intense anguish. Despite religious warnings, romance and love flourish in exile as well as throughout the mountains, valleys, and vast grasslands of Tibet.

Aten, the seventy-year-old Khampa freedom fighter, recalls courting in the old days. "My grandfather used to say that in Nyarong, girls would give their bootstraps to the boys they liked. Many men proudly sported half a dozen of these romantic tokens, much to the envy of friends and the grief and embarrassment of

indignant sweethearts." Tsering Lhamo from Amdo recalls that at the summer horse festivals girls would toss their hair ribbons to the riders on whom they had crushes. The riders then had their choice of the girls they wished to sleep with among those whose ribbons they had garnered.

Trinley Wangdu, another Khampa freedom fighter, recalls some of the seductive gestures made between prospective lovers: "A man would stroke his cheek with his forefinger or tug his ear, and if a woman responded in kind, they'd spend the night together." Mimicking *mudras*—esoteric religious hand gestures made by monks and yogins—lovers employed symbolic hand signals with meanings decidedly unreligious. In Kham, a man would discreetly slip his hand up the long sleeve of a prospective lover and caress her palm with a subtle gesture signaling a secret rendezvous later that night. Such unspoken proposals are still very common.

Even ancient codes of chivalry and romance dating back to Tibet's pre-Buddhist warrior culture sometimes still apply. Should a man from a feuding tribe tug his ear at a Khampa's chosen woman or dare to reach his hand up her sleeve, the Khampa lover may feel obliged to slay the man simply as a matter of honor.

Around the Barkhor, the central marketplace in Lhasa, bands of Khampa boys strut around in tall leather boots, swords dangling jauntily at their sides, their hair braided and wound around their heads with red and black tassels and adorned with thick ivory rings. Their cocky manner is calculated to impress bands of women from the town of Derge in Kham with whom they barter and flirt. These women, their braided hair strung with small turquoise stones, coyly sell fake coral, amber, and turquoise to unsuspecting tourists.

Among the nomads, the art of tea making is keenly observed by potential suitors, who court a girl at her parents' tent. Customarily, the suitor—like any other guest—is served Tibetan tea, which requires mixing butter, milk, tea, salt, and soda in a large wooden tea churn. Discreetly watching the girl as she churns the tea with a plunging motion, a suitor is said to assess his compatibility with her not by the quality of the tea but rather by the rhythm of her movements as she makes it.

When a courtship goes awry, sometimes all that remains are love's bleeding wounds. Dechen Lhamo unfolds worn love letters and bitterly recounts her story. Dashing and prominent, twenty-four-year-old Detong Tulku had a bevy of girls competing to be his secret consort. The most eligible incarnation in the refugee settlement, his prestigious spiritual ancestry maintains a centuries-old reputation for prowess in the transformative practices of sexual yoga.

"At first I thought he was just a playboy lama," Dechen Lhamo says. "Then I fell in love and I wanted nothing more than to practice the Dharma with him. We eloped and secretly got married." But Detong Tulku's family had other plans for him. Disregarding his marriage to Dechen, they arranged a formal marriage for him with a distant cousin, dashing all of Dechen's hopes for a life of Tantric connubial bliss. Among the aristocratic and religious lineages, "bone lines" are far more important than true love. Dechen's misfortune in love propelled her to seek solace in Buddhism, and she threw herself into religious retreat for over a year. "I never want to marry," she says. "I only want to practice the Dharma."

Luckily for Detong Tulku, Dechen chose not to avenge herself, unlike the Golok warriors of eastern Tibet, who, if wronged in love, traditionally sliced off the nose of the unfaithful lover. Love with attachment, the Buddhists say, and you will suffer and cause suffering. Playing with the fire of desire and passion can be dangerous. Unless of course, one knows how.

THE SPIRITUAL ART OF LOVE

Beggars frown on gold,
and hungry ghosts spit on food.
Sex is disclaimed by all,
but it alone
is what is liked
from the minds of all.
—Gedun Chöpel

Tibet abounds with great spiritual masters who reached profound realization through meditative practices founded on sexual energy and bliss. Making love can be an unexcelled, if perilous, spiritual path. Sexual experience among Tibetans ranges from the nonexistent to the crude to the sublime. An earthy warrior past intermingles with the influences of transcendental Buddhist philosophy and Tantric methodologies, in which passions are not rejected but embraced and transformed.

The Dalai Lama describes it this way: the Theravada Buddhists, who claim to follow the Buddha's teachings most precisely, approach passion as a poison to the mind that must be avoided at all costs. For the Mahayana Buddhists, who strive to liberate not only themselves but all beings, passion is a poison that can be cured with the antidote of compassion and wisdom. But Tibetan Tantric Buddhists, who view all life as inherently sacred, conceive of passion as a potent force that can be consumed and transformed. Just as a peacock can eat poisonous plants and transform them into the radiant colors of his feathers, a skillful Tantric Buddhist can transform passion into a elixir of long life.

Sensual depictions of deities in ecstatic sexual embrace abound in monasteries and family homes throughout Tibet and in exile. Referring to the Tantric path of inner transformation, these graphic images are not painted to induce erotic thoughts. Rather, they symbolize the spiritual union of radiant wisdom and the methods by which it is brought forth. The term for deities in sexual embrace—*yabyum*—is the honorific word for one's own parents: *yab* (father) and *yum* (mother). As a religious concept yabyum refers to the highest possible bliss: the union of *yum*, the transcendent wisdom or insight into Emptiness, with *yab*, the skillful means needed to reach enlightenment.

As Lama Thubten Yeshe explains: "Tantra recognizes the powerful energy aroused by our desires to be an indispensable resource for the spiritual path . . . What Tantra has to teach us is a way of breaking free from all the conditioning that limits our understanding of who we are and what we can become."

A group of militant performers from the Tibetan Institute of Performing Arts surround a portrait of the Dalai Lama in Darjeeling, India. TIPA is dedicated to preserving and disseminating Tibet's cultural heritage. During the 1980s Jamyang Norbu, one of the foremost Tibetan intellectuals in exile, encouraged TIPA to perform contemporary theatrical works. This idea encountered strong opposition among the more conservative elements of Tibetan society.

Tibetans protesting the Chinese occupation of Tibet at a March 10 demonstration, Darjeeling, India. "The Tibetan youth's biggest struggle is for freedom. In every Tibetan person's heart this is the struggle. I can't guarantee that all Tibetans will return if Tibet gets its freedom, but I am sure most of them will go."
—RAPTEN DORJE (ATEN), KHAMPA FREEDOM FIGHTER

Every March 10 Tibetans in exile demonstrate against the Chinese occupation
of their homeland. These young monks have gathered on the streets of
Darjeeling, India, to voice their protest.

Members of the Tibetan Institute of
Performing Arts on tour in Darjeeling.

Dressed in regal Khampa finery, Dorje Phuntsok sits in front of a portrait of his father, Lardor Rinpoche, and the Panchen Lama. Dorje Phuntsok grew up in Switzerland and works in Zurich as an interior designer. But he often visits his father, who returned to Kanze, Tibet, in 1983 to aid the Panchen Lama in development projects. "Tibetans in exile call my father a traitor for returning to Tibet," Dorje Phuntsok says. "But as a refugee in Switzerland my father worked in a factory. He was a nobody. He believed he could be of more help to his people by returning and working within the Chinese system."

"All the girls in Kanze dream of marrying Dorje Phuntsok and moving to Switzerland," admits Pema Choden. "My father was a monk who supplied guns to the Khampa freedom fighters and was imprisoned by the Chinese before being forced to marry my mother when he was fifty-six years old. My brother has tried escaping to India six times. I want to go too. Please take me with you." (Photograph by Ian Baker)

CELIBACY AND MARRIED MONKS

How could a civilization that celebrates sexually embracing deities have fostered such a large number of supposedly celibate monks and nuns? The Tantric path is considered the fastest, shortest, and most direct path to enlightenment. But just as taking the most direct route to the top of a mountain is fraught with danger for anyone but the most experienced climbers, Tantra is potentially dangerous for all but the most skilled and discerning practitioners. To avoid this danger, most monks and nuns tread a safer, more orthodox path to enlightenment, which includes following strict monastic rules, among them the vow of celibacy. Nevertheless, homosexuality, though frowned upon, is not unknown. Tashi, an ex-*dob-dob*—a member of the brutish monk security force at Ganden Monastery—writes, "It is true that their [*dob-dob*] fights were often about favorite boys, but what else could be expected in a community of only men and boys?"

Conversely, certain Tibetan Buddhist sects have a tradition of married lamas. Nyingmapa monks, for example, can choose either to take the vow of celibacy or to become a *nakpa*—a yogin or yogini who, as part of the path to liberation, may engage in the physically and psychically demanding practices of sexual yoga. Practicing with a qualified consort, yogins and yoginis retain and rechannel their semen and ovum fluids, using the resultant bliss (considered one hundred times greater than ejaculation) as a vital support for insight into Emptiness and ultimately as a direct path to enlightenment. The fluids and subtle essences aroused during the sexual act are esoterically considered the essence of *bodhicitta* (the force of awakening) and are therefore not to be squandered indiscriminately.

When I teased one of my Tibetan girlfriends about an illicit affair she was having with a supposedly celibate monk from a monastery in Boudha, Nepal, she turned to me with a straight face and said, "But don't you know about inner, outer, and secret celibacy? Outer celibacy, like the Theravada Buddhist view of passion, is to avoid sex completely. Inner celibacy is everything but penetration. And secret celibacy is penetration without ejaculation."

For Tantric yogins and yoginis, sexual practice can lead to more than physical well-being. Properly performed, it ensures longevity and develops clarity and insight. Spiritual revelations called *terma*—wisdom treasures of the earth, sky, and mind—are often revealed through sexual yoga. When Dilgo Khyentse Rinpoche became ill during his celibate youth, he was encouraged to take a consort in order to prolong his life. He did so and as a result lived until the ripe old age of eighty-one, receiving many visionary mind treasures.

EARTHY SEX

While sex for the spiritually adept is filled with transcendent possibilities, the sexual heritage of most lay Tibetans leans more toward the earthy. On a pragmatic level, Tibetan doctors consider an active sex life important for good health. One Tibetan medical text recommends the following schedule for sexual intercourse:

Two to three times a day in winter
Every two days in spring and autumn
Once every fifteen days in summer.

In his Tibetan classic *Treatise on Passion* (1938), Gedun Chöpel encourages "rough and playful sex," even advising sexual partners to pinch hard enough with their fingernails to leave deep red marks on breasts and buttocks, for "it is said that until the wounds heal and disappear, the enjoyment of passion is not forgotten."

Elements of the pre-Buddhist culture of Tibet continue to influence Tibetan sexuality. Pema, a former monk, tells of a Khampa custom called "outwitting the dog." A gang of boys picks a female victim—often a young shepherdess living in a tent in the highlands. When the girl is home alone, save for a fierce guard dog, the boys will 'outwit the dog' and brutally rape the girl in turns. The girl, too embarrassed and humiliated by the experience, will rarely utter a word against her assailants.

In the refugee camps, sexual activity starts at a young age. Yangzum, a young woman from Kham told me: "You will be washing dishes and a man will look at you or say, 'I'll be by tonight,' and then that night he sneaks through the window and crawls into bed with you. Your parents are sleeping next to you in the same room. It's no big deal. Once, my sister didn't like the boy who told her he was coming, so she asked our widowed aunt to sleep where my sister always sleeps. The boy came in the window and didn't find out until later he'd slept with our old aunt instead of my sister!"

A young aristocrat of Choni and his fourteen-year-old bride in their finest silk clothes and jewelry. The prince wears a fox-fur hat and a chuba trimmed with leopard fur.

Tashi Phuntsok, a handsome young Tibetan from the Dhorpatan refugee camp in rural Nepal, says: "If you say to a girl you're going to come over that night, and then you don't and you meet her the next day and she says, 'What, were you afraid?' then you know she really wants you to come. If you send her presents and she sends them back, that doesn't necessarily mean she doesn't like you. Just like our custom of refusing tea the first time it's offered to us, even if we really want it, a girl will often refuse you the first time, just to show she isn't easy to get."

MARRIAGE

"As a flower has a time to blossom, a woman has a time for marriage. As a flower withers and dies, a woman becomes old and can no longer marry. It is time for your marriage." With those words, my twenty-five-year-old friend Yangzum's mother let her know that against Yangzum's wishes, she had arranged for her to be married to a boy from a prestigious family in Boudha, Nepal. Long ago it was customary not even to let the bride know about her impending marriage. The mother traditionally told the matchmakers that her daughter was ugly and clumsy—in other words, she was so valuable that her mother was reluctant to part with her. Yangzum's suitors had a lama check her horoscope to see if the elements in her chart were in harmony with the prospective groom's. Born in the year of the dragon, Yangzum was considered a good catch who would bring prosperity and harmony to the home. Arranged marriages are the norm among aristocrats, nomadic chieftains, and prominent religious lineages, although today marriage for love is more common.

Whereas Tibetan Buddhists regard sex as filled with spiritual potential, they consider marriage and divorce essentially secular affairs, surprisingly lacking in Buddhist significance. This in no way dampens the wedding drama, however.

Tibetans in the remote Himalayas still follow the tradition of polyandry—the marriage of one woman to all the brothers in a family. Bedecked in silk brocade and adorned with magnificent hunks of turquoise, coral, pearl, and gold jewelry, the shy bride, surrounded by her young grooms, hides sullenly in the shadows beneath mounds of white blessing scarves, while dancers sway and sing wedding riddles in the cold Himalayan air until their voices are hoarse and the light of dawn emerges over the mountains. In this

area of western Tibet and northwestern Nepal, wedding ceremonies reenact the marriage of the great seventh-century king Srongsten Gampo to the Chinese princess Wen Chen Konjo in a five-day, operalike spectacle.

At Yangzum's wedding in Kathmandu, the guests gambled and played cards in a huge cement-block hall. After the elder generation's high-pitched singing and exuberant stomping had ebbed, kids in Hong Kong imitation duds began to break-dance to the driving beat of Madonna. Yangzum looked unhappy, as an obedient bride should. If she had displayed happiness upon leaving her family, she would not only have insulted her parents, but might also have enticed the luck of her family to leave with her. Hunched beside her groom behind a low-lying table, her face was completely obscured by a gold-embroidered brocade hat trimmed with muskrat fur and a huge mound of presents, blessing scarves, and envelopes of money.

In old Tibet, marital relations could become quite complex. It was not uncommon for a man to marry two or three sisters, or two sisters to be married to five brothers, or a father and son or a mother and daughter to share a spouse. With marriage customs as diverse as the regions of Tibet, I was not surprised that Yangzum and her groom decided not to exchange pieces of turquoise and gold, which would have symbolized the union of their souls (*lha*), nor that they did not follow the ancient Bon tradition of attaching a woolen sky cord to the groom and a blue prosperity cord to the bride. This tradition is based on the myth of the marriage of the goddess Sri Kamtrulmoche to the mortal Lingkar, who persuaded the goddess's father to let a human marry his divine daughter. Lingkar argued that the sun and moon remain in the sky, yet their rays fall on earth and in return earth's vapors rise to the sky; so too the union of gods and men, he contended, would be no less mutually beneficial: humans would respect the gods and the gods would provide humans with protection. The goddess's father reluctantly consented and gave Kamtrulmoche a divine arrow, symbolic of her life force and her divine origins. Her mother gave her a spindle and her brother gave her turquoise. When the different cords are attached to the bride and groom, a lama recites:

May the arrow of manhood and the spindle of women
remain united. May the sky and prosperity cords remain
uncut. May the union of gods and men remain firm.

The Spiritual Art of Love—Tantric Deities in Ecstatic Union, thangka painting. "The function of Tantra is to transform all pleasures into the transcendental experience of deep penetrative awareness. Instead of advocating separation from worldly pleasures . . . Tantra channels the energy of enjoyment into a quick and powerful path to fulfillment and enlightenment. This is the most skillful way of using our precious human potential."
—LAMA YESHE

A young bride in Limi, northern Nepal, stands next to her three new husbands.
Following tradition, the marriage is a five-day operalike affair during which
riddles testing the worthiness of the grooms' clan are sung. The ceremony itself
is a reenactment of the marriage of the seventh-century Tibetan king Srongsten
Gampo to his Chinese bride, Wen Chen Konjo.

A young bride rises from her sheepskin bed for a cup of salt-butter tea. Mount Kailas region, western Tibet.

O that the one who has
entered my heart
might be my lifelong companion!
It would be like gaining a precious
  gem
from the depths of the
  ocean.
      —THE SIXTH DALAI LAMA

This ten-year-old bride is bedecked in jewelry symbolizing the wealth and prosperity she brings to her new household. The silver and gold *gaous* around her neck are portable altars to protect her from spirits at this vulnerable time in her life— between leaving the gods of her home and pledging her allegiance to the gods of her husband's home. After the ceremony, she will return to her parents' home until she reaches puberty. "I don't want to get married," she admits. "I'd rather stay in my parents' home and be with my friends. But what can I do? I must obey my parents."

At a wedding ceremony in Kathmandu, Nepal, lavishly dressed guests bestow blessings on the parents as well as on the bride and groom. In Tibet, marriage took a variety of forms, including polyandry, polygamy, polygyny, and monogamy. Mother and daughter sometimes shared husbands, and father and son sometimes shared wives. For Tibetan Buddhists, marriage is considered a secular affair with little religious significance.

In an ancient Bon myth about the origin of marriage, the primordial princess bride must gamble with her brothers for her share of family property. Her brothers win, however, so she must forfeit her right to an inheritance. Ever since, gambling has been an integral part of Tibetan weddings. The guests spend most of the day at the gambling tables; the stakes are high, and small fortunes are lost and won. Even monks—inveterate gamblers—join in.

Love blooms backstage at the Tibetan Institute of Performing Arts,
Dharamsala, India.

ADULTHOOD

WAYS OF LIVING

NATURAL RHYTHMS

Among Tibetans, work knows few boundaries when it comes to age. I have seen little girls hauling sloshing buckets from faraway springs and slicing turnips late into the evening, while old withered men with needle in hand industriously patched worn cloth boots. From the slate-gray darkness before dawn until far past dusk, Tibetans can be found hard at work. Sheep need shearing, *drimo* (female yaks) need milking, shop doors need opening, crops need harvesting, wool needs spinning, texts need reading, lamps need lighting, prayers need praying. The tasks of everyday living are endless.

Industrious and resourceful, Tibetans consider work as natural a part of life as breathing. "We work to live," eighty-year-old Eppi told me while picking burrs off her lone cow. "Without work, how can we survive?" She took for granted the notion that work and spiritual pursuits were one. As she spun her mani wheel with one hand and stirred dinner with the other, she would hum mantras. For Eppi, work was an extended form of prayer, no matter how mundane the task.

For those who choose the married path, the work of rearing and providing for one's family takes precedence. There are babies to be rocked, lullabies to be sung, and children to be caressed, reprimanded,

Sheep and yaks graze along the shore of Lake Namtso. In the distance are the snow-dusted Nyenchen Tanglha Mountains. "In the spring, when the ice cracks and melts, we say the sounds are the mountain spirits performing sacred ceremonies at Nyenchen Tanglha. The Chinese can't prevent the mountain spirits' ceremonies, now can they?"
—LHENDROP, NOMADIC MONK

clothed, and fed. "Without children, who will take care of us when we are old?" Dekyi Wangmo, a mother of six, tells me. "A house with no children is a house full of sorrow." In old Tibet it was common for many brothers to share one wife. The daily work of marriage and family life was compounded by the need to keep a household free of jealousy and discord. "My work is to maintain harmony," says Ang Zangmo, the wife of five brothers.

TRADER INSTINCTS

For the father of a family, the work of providing often necessitates extended travel. We awoke one July morning to find a thick carpet of snow on the ground and a tremendous caravan of Changtang salt traders with over a hundred yaks trudging by our tent on their way north to the salt plains, an excursion that would keep them away from home for over six weeks. An old Tibetan saying maintains, "If religion is the heart of the Tibetan people, then trade is most surely her lungs." Indeed, trade has traditionally been the bellows of the Tibetan economy. Living on the roof of the world, Tibetans are natural traders who barter by instinct. It is not surprising that archaeologists have found Tibetan coins as far away as ancient Greece, where early Tibetan traders presumably wandered in search of a good deal.

Traveling vast distances to the courts of emperors and khans in neighboring China and Mongolia or south to the palaces of the great moguls and rajas in India, Tibetans were notoriously clever when bartering their salt, wool, horses, butter, sheep, and yak tails for Chinese silk, porcelain, and bricks of tea, or for Indian spices, cloth, jewels, and coveted Buddhist scriptures.

BANDITS AND BRIGANDS

The traders who crossed the vast Tibetan plateau in enormous caravans laden with foreign goods attracted others to more scurrilous yet no less profitable professions: banditry and highway robbery. Near the great pilgrimage sites, such as Mount Kailas in western Tibet, whole clans of proud bandits and brigands routinely plundered caravans, excising from them what they felt was their due as a "tax" for traveling in their territory. In eastern Tibet, attacking caravans was the full-time occupation of many Golok tribesmen, who boasted that their "work" displayed their courage and warrior skills. Buddhist scripture invoking "right livelihood"—the need to earn a living through honest hard work involving no stealing, cheating, or lying—is blatantly ignored by karma-laden criminals who continue to ply their dubious trade. In 1990 a small gang was caught stealing a life-size statue from the Sera Monastery in Tibet. They had cleverly wrapped the Buddha figure in a burial cloth and carried it as if it were a corpse to be cremated on a distant hill, where their getaway truck was waiting for them. Gold smugglers resort to divine protection when sneaking gold from Hong Kong into Nepal. While chanting protective Tara mantras at the airport, they visualize the protectress sewing shut the eyes of the customs officials as they pass.

FARMERS AND NOMADS

Archaeologists surmise that farming was not widely practiced in Tibet until two thousand years ago, when Tibetans began adopting patterns of cereal agriculture identical to those of the Sumerians and Phoenicians of the Near East. As early as 3000 B.C. a pastoral, nomadic way of life had developed on the Tibetan steppes, with warriorlike nomads raiding the more peaceable settled farmers. Contact between nomads and farmers has always been necessary as farmers need the nomads' dairy and meat products, and the nomads need the farmers' grain. "We farmers have the wealth of the land, but nomads have the wealth of butter and yogurt," an old Utsang Province farmer told us. He lives beside the Tsangpo River, the source of Tibet's earliest civilizations.

Before the 1950 Chinese invasion, Tibetan society consisted of nomads, farmers, aristocratic landowners, government officials, peasants, and merchants, while approximately one-third of the population resided in monasteries as monks and nuns.

MONASTIC WORK

Buddha technically forbade monks from involvement in commerce, but in Tibet many monks resorted to seasonal trade to help support themselves. Kesang Choda, an ex-monk, recalls: "There were certain times during the year when we would have to be in the monastery. Other times, we'd be free, so we'd go on business trips." Rich monks were allowed to possess property and servants, while poorer monks sustained themselves through agricultural work, cooking in the large monastic kitchens, assisting in the preparation of ritual offerings, or playing ritual musical instruments during ceremonies. Typical monastic activities included carving woodblocks for prayers, filling chortens with sacred substances, sculpting barley *tormas* for altars, carving butter statues, executing elaborate sand mandalas, performing prostrations, chanting mantras, and, in rhythm with the waning and waxing moon, gathering for ceremonies dedicated to specific deities. Sometimes less spiritually inclined monks chose to work as dob-dobs—rough, belligerent monks who policed the monasteries and huge monastic festivals.

Most village lamas restricted themselves to the pragmatic work of their profession—attending to the omnipresent cycle of life: blessing and naming infants, drawing up astrological charts, keeping evil away from marriages, performing house blessings and exorcisms, offering prayers for good luck and long life, and aiding the dying and deceased through the bardo—the transitional realm between this life and the next.

LIBERATION IN DAILY LIFE

For devout practitioners, every chore or activity, no matter how mundane, is a stepping stone to spiritual liberation. Prayer and work become one as each solitary act of labor is expanded to include all sentient beings. Simple practitioners are taught to enhance their daily work with spiritually significant sayings. "As I open this barn door, may I release all those suffering in hell realms. As I light this lantern, may it shine the light of the Dharma on all suffering beings. Chopping wood, may I cut through the illusion of permanence. Washing my hands, may I wash away the ignorance of dualistic vision from the minds of all suffering beings." Such aphorisms are particularly popular in the Gelugpa school of Tibetan Buddhism, but, as Tulku Orgyen, the great Nyingma meditation master, urges, we must ultimately go beyond all such conceptual formulations to the source of true awakening, asking ourselves, "Who is the one opening the barn door? Who is the one lighting the lamp?"

SCHOLARS AND ARTISANS

Tibetan monasteries, acting essentially as universities and centers of learning, fostered the development of artisans and scholars. The great early scholars worked on translating the entire corpus of Buddhist doctrine from the original Sanskrit. Later scholars wrote commentaries, while debaters with warriorlike gestures vigorously argued opposing doctrines and philosophical viewpoints. Monasteries such as Derge flourished as printing presses of Buddhist scripture, Tibet's first books. In addition to religion and philosophy, other disciplines, including medicine, pharmacology, astronomy, and astrology, thrived amid the intense intellectual ferment of the monasteries.

Influenced by Kashmiri, Khotanese, Newari, and Chinese styles, monasteries and wealthy patrons commissioned painters and sculptors to create images of great saints and spiritual masters, as well as to give bold anthropomorphic form to heightened states of awareness. Practitioners use these paintings, known as *thangkas,* and sculptures as sources of inspiration on their path toward liberation.

TRAVELING PROFESSIONS

As in medieval Europe, traveling entertainers—musicians, storytellers, actors, acrobatic troupes, opera troupes, and bards—freely wandered the countryside, entertaining in small village hamlets until the Chinese invasion in 1950. Traveling bards recited the Gesar epics in a trancelike state and told stories of yogins with magical powers in faraway lands. Mendicants, soothsayers, diviners, healers, mystics, oracles, yogins, weathermen, charlatans, robbers, and professional beggars pursued their vocations along bustling pilgrim routes.

WORK OF THE YOGINS

In remote caves and rock shelters far above the fortresslike monastic cities, nomadic encampments, adobe-style Tibetan villages, and refugee settlements of India and Nepal, the few remaining hermit yogins who have survived Chinese persecution continue working diligently toward liberation. Their reclusive labors may produce nothing externally tangible, but most Tibetans believe that a good hermit's daily practices and solitary prayers for peace are substantially more beneficial than the arduous physical labor of even the most ambitious layman. Tibet's great saint Milarepa, who lived in rock shelters with only a few possessions, wore simple cotton clothing, and left his hair wild and matted, said, "When ordinary people look at me they feel pity, but when the enlightened masters regard me they are overjoyed," for despite his humble physical appearance and lack of material wealth, through sheer devoted practice his mind was one with the Buddhas.

Meditating beside thundering waterfalls, atop steep cliffs, or in cremation grounds at night, selflessly offering their physical body to conjured ghosts and demons, yogins and yoginis following the tradition of Chöd strive to abandon fear and realize their innermost nature of clear, radiant light. Bonpo and Nyingmapa practitioners of *muntri*—dark retreat—are boarded up in pitch-black caves, often for three years or more, seeking the experience of the luminous light beyond birth and death that abides latently within all beings. Other yogins—with or without consorts—meditate on the subtle channels, inner winds, and energy centers within the body, often simulating the experiences of death and the bardo. Through yogic breathing, dream practices, and complex visualizations of Tantric deities, yogins work to penetrate beyond the illusions of this life and gain insight and awareness that may help release all suffering beings from the wheel of cyclic existence. Ultimately, the *naljorpa,* as the yogin is called in Tibetan, discovers that the greatest work of life is to cease striving and "rest with joy in the Natural State," as the word *naljor* implies.

The last light of day silhouettes a young shepherd heading home with his flock, Utsang, Tibet.

In the pastures of Great Bliss,
I was herding Immortal Sheep;
I had no time to watch
Those of blood and flesh.
                    —MILAREPA

A July snowstorm in the Lake Namtso region blankets the terrain without halting a yak caravan headed to the salt flats farther north. Yaks are probably the most useful animal on earth. Their skins are made into grain bags and the soles of boots. Their hair is spun into tent ropes and woven into tents. Their horns are made into containers for liquids, and the tip of the horn is often embossed with silver and used to carry snuff. Yak bones are used to build houses. Their backbones were traditionally crushed and mixed with gold dust to make a female contraceptive. The yak's heart is believed to be effective medicine for heart trouble and Tibetans eat it to increase their courage.

Illuminated by the last rays of the setting sun, this flock of sheep suggests their sacred counterparts, who live in heaven and whose fleecy coats we mistake for clouds in the sky. South-central Tibet.

Nuns at the Tatsang Nunnery. Their heads are covered with yak-tail wig hats, traditionally worn for warmth and protection from the rain, as well as for travel outside the nunnery compound.

A nun's life is not all work and prayer. These nuns are bathing in a sacred pool at the Tirdrom retreat center in central Tibet, where the great saint Padmasambhava and his consort Yeshe Tsogyal are said to have bathed during their seven-year retreat together. Yeshe Tsogyal obtained enlightenment here and said, "I don't ever want to leave this place." As a result, she is believed to return here on the tenth and twenty-fifth day of every lunar month. The current incarnation of Yeshe Tsogyal lives at a nearby hermitage and continues to frequent this pool.

Gold miners near Derge, eastern Tibet.
"Long ago, the sacred *lu* (snakelike beings
of the underworld) ate the fruit of a
precious tree, and their excrement turned
to gold and that is the gold we still find
in the earth today."
—JIGME NORBU

But the deities of the land do not always
approve of gold extraction and sometimes
the lu can become angry. In the 1920s mining was halted in a gold mine near Mount
Kailas when an outbreak of measles was
reported. After forty years of forced labor
in Chinese mines, Tibetans are less concerned with disturbing deities than with
survival. Prospectors must give a portion of
their findings to the government for the
right to work the mines.

Loggers in Nyarong, eastern Tibet. Tibet's forests constitute the largest forest
reserve at China's disposal. Fifty-four billion dollars' worth of Tibetan
timber—25 percent of its forests—has been cut in the last thirty years, and,
according to a Chinese survey in 1990, there was only a six-year supply
of accessible timber left to log. "When I was young, Nyarong was known for
its thick, rich forests. Now whole mountainsides have been stripped bare."
—CHIME DORJE

Like a procession of ants, Chinese trucks loaded with
Tibetan timber make their way to China along the
precariously winding roads carved out of the Szechuan
hills. "Destruction of nature and natural resources
results from ignorance, greed, and lack of respect for
the earth's living things. . . . It is not difficult to forgive
destruction in the path which resulted from ignorance.
Today, however, we have access to more information,
and it is essential that we re-examine ethically what we
have inherited, what we are responsible for, and what
we will pass on to coming generations."
—TENZIN GYATSO, THE FOURTEENTH DALAI LAMA

Trogawa Rinpoche, a prominent Tibetan medical doctor in Kathmandu, diagnoses a patient by reading his eighteen different pulses, a skill believed to take more than a decade to master. According to Tibetan medicine, the fundamental cause of all bodily illness is *marigpa*—ignorance of our own basic nature. This ignorance creates passion, aggression, and stupidity, which in turn affect the harmony of the body's inner winds.

An incense maker, Kalimpong, India. Tibetan refugees in exile have worked
hard to create decent lives amid India's pervasive poverty. Incense is
commonly used by Tibetans to purify the environment and to summon
and please deities. Different deities are pleased by different scents, and the
ingredients of the incense vary accordingly.

TIBET TODAY

In feudal Tibet, the entire countryside was seen as a sacred realm belonging to the Dalai Lama, Chenresrig incarnate, the patron deity of Tibet and the divine ruler at the center of Tibet's mandala. Tribute and devotion were paid to this divine center in return for protection and blessing. Aristocrats, who owned huge estates worked by peasants, were required to pay taxes in the form of grain and animals to the Dalai Lama's central government. Monasteries paid tribute in the form of prayers and rituals, and nomads who did not graze their herds on monastery-owned land were required to offer butter and meat, in addition to providing army and escort services for government officials passing through their territory.

When I listen to the tales of precommunist Tibet, I cannot help but share the Dalai Lama's convictions that Tibet was a feudalistic society in dire need of reform. Corruption and abuse of power among the aristocracy and ruling theocracy were rampant. One monk at Kathok Monastery in eastern Tibet told me, "At least the Chinese don't tax us the way the monasteries used to." The Chinese have built extensive roads and electrified many towns. Yet, when examined closely, it becomes evident that this material progress has been made not for the benefit of the local Tibetans but primarily for the Chinese military and the influx of Chinese settlers. It is difficult to believe Chinese claims that the invasion and occupation of Tibet in the 1950s was truly to liberate Tibet from the shackles of feudalism and not to plunder the "Western Treasure House" for the material benefit of the Chinese state.

Literally thousands of Tibetans today toil in Chinese forced-labor camps. The majority of workers continue to be nomads and farmers. There is virtually no manufacturing in the country. The only established industries are cement, wood, fertilizer, and sugar. Fertilizer alone is produced for Tibet; all other raw materials are trucked to China. Landowners have simply been replaced by the state. Stripped of their spiritual and sacred center, the Dalai Lama, Tibetans must now work like serfs not for a divine ruling power but for the material progress of the totalitarian Chinese government. There are rumors that Tibet may someday become an economic free zone, but until a radical change in policy occurs in Beijing, those toiling in work camps, mining borax in the Changtang, and logging in the forests of Kongpo and Kham have little hope for significant reform.

CHINESE SETTLERS AND UNEMPLOYMENT

Tibetans who are not in forced-labor camps are lucky to find work. An estimated 7.5 million Chinese live in Tibet, compared to 6 million Tibetans. In Lhasa, Chinese outnumber Tibetans three to one. Lured to Tibet with government offers of three times their normal wages, migrating Chinese settlers caused the unemployment rate in the Lhasa Valley to skyrocket to 70 percent in 1992. Not unlike the Native Americans of the United States, Tibetans are increasingly marginalized in their own country. Since all official business is conducted in Chinese, discriminatory policies pervade employment practices.

As Jamyang Norbu, a writer and former director of the Tibetan Institute of Performing Arts, writes, "Chinese carpenters, masons, tailors, petty traders, restaurateurs, truck drivers, teachers, electricians, mechanics, barbers, butchers, guides, street entertainers, beggars, and of course the myriad ubiquitous functionaries so indispensable to the proper functioning of a totalitarian state, are relentlessly pushing Tibetans into immediate unemployment and ultimate extinction."

EXILE

When the Dalai Lama escaped from Tibet in 1959, nearly a hundred thousand Tibetans followed him across the Himalayas into exile. They followed him on faith, with little but the clothes on their backs. By toiling in road crews to build Indian highways, buying bright, cheap sweaters and hawking them on the streets of Calcutta and Bombay, and clearing the jungle in southern India to raise crops, they carved out an existence on unwanted land in one of the poorest, most densely populated countries in the world. Determined to preserve what the Chinese were destroying in their native land, the Tibetans began reconstructing their monasteries, the repositories of their faith. In 1959, twenty thousand monks belonged to the Drepung, Sera, and Ganden monasteries in central Tibet. Today, eight thousand monks are enrolled in the newly built Indian versions of these same institutions.

FROM REFUGEES TO CARPET BARONS

Illiterate and clothed in rags, the Tibetan refugees in Nepal needed help and it was their carpets that came to the rescue. "Within three years," says Father Moran, founding member of the Nepal

International Tibetan Refugee Committee, "the refugees had forsaken the dark and dirty tents of the Jawalakhel settlement, wore wristwatches, and were living in rented rooms."

What began as a modest handicraft operation by distraught refugees has grown into a full-fledged commercial enterprise. No business earns more money for Nepal than the production of Tibetan carpets; it contributes nearly seventy million dollars a year to the coffers of this impoverished Himalayan kingdom. Tibetans own 70 percent of the carpet factories, which employ more than three hundred thousand workers. But, despite impressive exports and job opportunities, the rug business has its problems. Most of the factory workers are Nepalese women under the age of sixteen who have fled to the city from the poverty-stricken hills. They labor an average of fourteen hours a day in the dreary, cramped, and poorly ventilated factories.

In 1991 importing agencies realized that the carpets could be chemically treated less expensively in Nepal than in the countries to which they were being exported. As a result, workers now handle hazardous acids and chemical dyes, while the dangerous, untreated effluents pollute the rivers and ground water of the Kathmandu Valley.

Within the competitive pursuit of greater profit margins, some Tibetans maintain an altruistic perspective about the purpose of their work. With prayer beads wrapped around his wrist, Jamyang Thupten, a thirty-eight-year-old businessman, patiently punches numbers into his calculator before graciously serving us a cup of steaming hot tea. His tone is humble, unpretentious, and genuine. "I work so I can support my brother, who was tortured and escaped from Tibet. I don't mind helping him because the work he does through prayers and meditation will help all sentient beings. He is doing the real work of life."

As night descends over India, Nepal, and Tibet, hoes are propped against shed walls, animals are bedded down, computers are turned off, looms are left, pots are scoured, muddy boots are pulled off aching feet, and all those, rich and poor, who have worked hard to earn their daily bread, can snuff out the light and sleep peacefully until dawn. It is at this time that the Dalai Lama looks up at the moon, the same moon that he knows is watching his people imprisoned in labor camps throughout Tibet, and he prays all through the night, even while sleeping, for the cessation of suffering. But for today, the hard labor of a day's work is done, and tomorrow beckons with the prospect of celebration.

A carpet factory worker peers out from behind drying skeins of dyed wool,
Kathmandu Valley, Nepal. Tibetan refugees in India accuse the successful
Tibetan carpet manufacturers in Nepal of thinking only of business.
Carpets destined for Germany are now chemically treated in Nepal.
Workers handle hazardous acids, and toxic chemicals pollute the rivers
and ground water of the Kathmandu Valley.

Some thirty years ago the first Tibetan carpets made for export in Nepal
were produced in the Jawalakhel settlement. Today most carpet-industry
workers are Nepalese. Jawalakhel is one of the few factories in Kathmandu
where Tibetans still work.

CELEBRATION

SEASONAL CYCLES

Linked in their origins to the occupational cycles of planting, harvesting, summer herding, and winter trade, festivals in Tibet are not so much departures from work and everyday life as celebrations of the fruits of collective labor and seasonal rites to ensure their continued success. Groups of men and women can often be found singing joyously while working in the fields or preparing the ground for planting. Many folk songs grew out of communal work, and traditional dances often mimic the rhythmic motions of threshing or reaping, celebrating the growth of the soil and the seasonal cycles that bring change and renewal to the land and community.

Many festivals are rooted in ancient customs and traditions associated with the bounty and fertility of the earth. When the crops have ripened—and customarily before the wild geese fly south for the winter—Tibetans gather in grassy meadows for communal picnics accompanied by dancing, singing, archery contests, horse racing, and folk operas called *ache lhamo*. Only after the sumptuous events and celebrations of the Wangkhor festival have concluded can harvesting begin.

Wangkhor literally means "making the rounds of the fields" and can be traced to ancient Bon rites in which villagers made a circuit of their fields led by a Bonpo priest who held in his hands a ritual

The sacred dances of Tibet unite the monastic and lay communities in revelry and celebration. Dressed in rich brocades and a rosette headdress, this dakini dancer at the Chongra summer festival in the Derge district of eastern Tibet represents the energy of passion transformed into ecstatic awareness. As Trungpa Rinpoche writes: "Such passion is immensely powerful, it radiates warmth in all directions. It simultaneously nurtures the welfare of beings and blazes through the neurotic tendencies of ego."

arrow wrapped in a five-colored ceremonial scarf, which he rotated over the earth to ensure the "luck of the soil" and a prosperous harvest. Honoring the warlike character of the Bon deities who protected the land and people, a series of martial contests followed, including wrestling, archery, and swordsmanship. To amuse the more beneficent *sadag*—the "lords of the soil"—singing and dancing went on into the night.

Instituted in the fifteenth century, the Monlam New Year's Festival was celebrated every year until the Chinese occupation of Tibet in the 1950s. During the three-week event, elaborate religious ceremonies were followed by military pageants, archery contests, and horse races. Each year young women such as these, lavishly dressed in silk brocades and jewelry, were selected to serve *chang* (barley beer) to spectators at the pageants.

With the arrival of Buddhism in the eighth century, the same rites continued, but along with the ritual arrow representing the life force of the tribe, statues of the Buddha were carried in the procession and the ancient invocations were embellished with Buddhist mantras. Over time Wangkhor, like other summer festivals such as Shoton (the Yogurt festival) and Bathing Week, focused less on sympathetic magic and more on secular amusements. The all-pervasive spirit of conviviality, however, maintained what was perhaps the festivals' primary function: renewing relationships with the land and with one another at the height of the year, when the fields of wheat and barley stood tall and golden under the early autumn sky.

SACRED TIME

For Tibetans, just as there are sacred places, so too are there sacred times—periods of the year infused with heightened energy and significance. Configurations of stars and planets influence every movement of Tibetans' lives. At times inauspicious conjunctions lead to the deletion of entire months from the Tibetan calendar. Alternatively, days or months are repeated when favorable conditions prevail between earth and sky.

The most sacred time of all—and simultaneously the most uncertain—is the birth of the new year in early spring. Losar, the Tibetan New Year, which begins with the rise of the new moon in our own month of February or March, is considered the greatest of Tibetan *duschen,* or "great times." Yet as a transitionary period between two cycles it is as ambiguous and precarious as the bardo— the interim between two lives.

With the same attention that would be given a newborn infant, rites are performed in the last days of the waning year to dispel obstacles and ensure a harmonious transition into the next cycle. At the domestic level, old debts are settled and homes cleaned and refurbished. The family's best carpets and finest silver cups and plates are set out and good luck signs are strategically placed on the walls. Each morning clouds of juniper smoke rise from the rooftops as family members invoke ancestral protector gods in the guise of Buddhist divinities. At the monasteries, monks perform ancient ceremonies to drive out the negative forces of the passing year. On the dark moon day dough effigies representing the collective evil and ill will of the past twelve months are ritually incinerated, reshaping through ceremonial rites the flow of time itself.

On the first day of the new year Tibetans traditionally rise before dawn and make offerings at the family shrine. One's actions on the first days of the new year set the course for the ensuing twelve months, and during the parties, feasts, and gaming events in which Losar abounds, Tibetans take vigilant care to avoid negative encounters or states of mind. As one Tibetan explains, "To quarrel, cry, or lose one's temper is regarded as most inauspicious, unlucky, and a sure sign of bad times to come."

On the third day of the new year the entire community gathers at a sacred prominence above the village or town and offers *lhasang*—the smoke of juniper, cedar, and other purifying herbs—to the celestial realm of Buddhas and ancestral gods. Recalling the columns of wind and light by which the first Tibetan kings descended from the sky, the blessings of the Buddhas—"the Awakened Ones"—descend from the heavens in the smoke of the ritual fires, offering guidance and protection to all beings. As the fragrant, swirling smoke rises and dissolves in the air like an apparition, celebrants read omens and portents of the coming year. Then suddenly, at a precise moment indicated by the officiating lama, amid the drone of great horns and the clanging of cymbals, great handfuls of *tsampa*, or ground barley—the refined essence of the bounty of the fields—are thrown toward the sky to shouts of "Lha gya lo!" (May the gods be victorious!), offering in recognition and appreciation the essence of what the gods themselves bestowed.

PASSION PLAYS

In many ways early Buddhist traditions in Tibet resembled ancient Bon practices, with the essential difference of recognizing the supreme divine principle not solely as an external force but as a latent potential within our innermost being. To develop an awareness of Buddhist principles outside the monastic setting, to teach fundamental tenets of the religion, and to show a path beyond ignorance, fear, and aggression, dance dramas were devised to commemorate events in the lives of Bodhisattvas and miracle-working saints such as Milarepa and Padmasambhava.

Padmasambhava—better known as Guru Rinpoche, "the Precious Teacher"—firmly established the teachings of Indian

Vajrayana, or Tantric Buddhism, on Tibetan soil in the eighth century A.D. Due to his capacity to adapt the Buddhist teachings to changing circumstances, Padmasambhava was credited with numerous manifestations celebrated each month in Tantric feast offerings on the tenth day of the new moon. Padmasambhava is often referred to as the second Buddha, yet like all Buddhist lineages in Tibet, his teachings are based on those of the historical Buddha, Sakyamuni, who lived in India in the fifth century B.C. The miraculous birth, enlightenment, and final passing into Nirvana of Sakyamuni Buddha are celebrated annually on the full moon day of the fourth Tibetan month. Like the passion plays of medieval Europe, the dramatic reenactments of Buddhist legends and tales

During the New Year's festivities in Lhasa crowds of people would congregate at the base of the Potala Palace to watch daring acrobatic feats. This performance on a fifty-foot-high pole replaced an earlier tradition of sliding down a yak-hair rope. The latter was discouraged by the Thirteenth Dalai Lama, who thought it excessively dangerous.

unite religious specialists and lay people alike in a common vision of a world renewed and transformed through spiritual intercession.

The greatest of Tibet's religious celebrations, sacred masked dances called *Cham*—attributed in their origins to Padmasambhava—form an essential part of many festivals throughout the year. Outwardly reenacting historical events associated with the vanquishing of evil and establishing of Buddhism in Tibet, these sacred dance ceremonies dramatize the transformation of turbulent psychic forces into the energies of wisdom and compassion.

As if harnessing the energy of the high winds that sweep down the surrounding mountains, the Cham ceremonies at Kathok Monastery in eastern Tibet begin with the drone of conch shells and twenty-foot gilt copper horns, which echo and reverberate across the valley. Black-hatted dancers in silk robes embroidered with skulls and flaming *vajras*—symbols of the adamantine path of Tantric Buddhism—emerge from the monastery *lhakhang,* or spirit house, and, to the sound of drums, horns, and clashing cymbals perform the Dance of Subjugation. Swirling in intricate, interconnected patterns, each dancer seems less an individual performer than an integral link in an unfolding mandala, a collective force subduing contrary influences and renewing the links between the gods and humankind.

Originally performed as secret Tantric rites to actualize inner meditative experience, Cham ceremonies have been performed publicly only since the fifteenth century. The democratization of the sacred dances initiated Tibet's lay population into mysteries once available only to monks and yogins, strengthening faith in the Buddhist teachings and popular support for the monasteries. Outwardly proclaiming the triumph of good over evil, the sacred dance ceremonies inwardly retain their esoteric function as rites of consecration and self-transformation. Many aspects of Cham are still performed only behind closed doors where, through a precise inner choreography, the initiate invokes in his or her own body the energies of the Tantric gods until the duality of dancer and dance dissolves in ecstatic movement.

Dramatizing inner psychic forces perceived initially as external, the masked dances reveal the artifice and inadequacy of lives bound by beliefs in a limited or inflexible identity. "The many masks the dancers wear," a lama in Nepal explains, "show us the diverse potential of our innermost being. . . . Wearing masks we come to recognize our true condition." From the Buddhist point of view the belief in the self as a fixed or separate entity is the root of all illusion. By heightening the illusion, or as Lama Sangwa suggests, by adopting masks, we can paradoxically unmask the original self, which is free, uninhibited, and capable of responding dynamically to all situations.

Unlike the lower Buddhist schools, in Tantra the passions that give rise to distortion and delusion are not rejected. Experienced as the radiant energy of enlightened mind itself, the passions are displayed as ornaments symbolized by the lavish costumes, crowns, and masks of the powerful Tantric deities. By uninhibitedly immersing ourselves in life and not recoiling from it, we awaken forces that urge us into a magical interweaving dance in which the passions conjoin with the penetrating clarity of primordial awareness.

SACRED CLOWNS

For all their pageantry, or perhaps because of it, the Cham ceremonies dramatically reveal subtle Buddhist truths and challenge our tendency to separate the sacred from the profane. As Tantric masters repeatedly warn, seriousness is one of the greatest barriers on the spiritual path. "Humorlessness is one way the ego habitually protects itself," says Lama Sangwa. "Everything gets very solid—the very opposite of awakened mind."

The clown figures and caricatured saints who parade on the edges of the Cham festivals mock audience and performers alike, preventing the sanctified environment from becoming too solemn. Taunting monks as well as members of the crowd with lewd and irreverent gestures, the divine clowns continuously parody the formalism of the religious rites, reminding us that the profoundest truths we can conceive are ultimately nothing but magical display. The humor and spontaneity of the clowns and trickster-saints arise from the attempt to see through form to the constructed nature of all phenomena. They remind us that not taking anything too seriously—especially ourselves—is the foundation of compassion and transcendental vision. Ultimately the sacred clowns and divine madmen teach us how to let go of religious formality and convention and relate freely and spontaneously with all life.

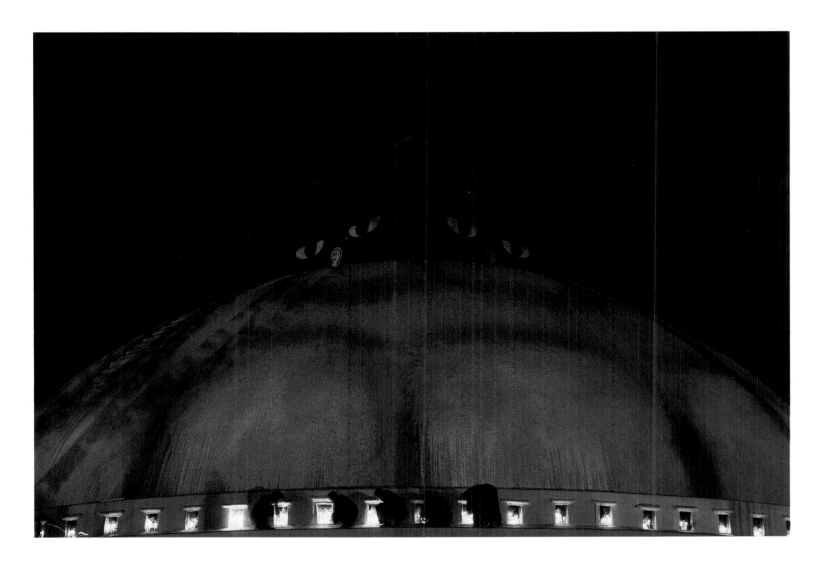

Losar celebrants offering lights at the Great Stupa at Boudhanath, Kathmandu Valley, Nepal. The Tibetan year ritually begins with the rise of the new moon in February. Activities performed at Losar establish patterns that will resonate throughout the coming year. As Ngakchang Sakya Sangpo proclaimed:

> *Whoever offers lamps to the Great Stupa*
> *Illuminates the darkness of unknowing. . . .*
> *All wishes will be granted and even*
> *Supreme realization and spiritual power may be attained.*

ABOVE
In a mountainous region of northern Kham, monks of Talok Monastery practice the Gesar dances that are performed during the annual summer festival.

OPPOSITE
At the end of the Cham ceremonies a gilded statue of Padmasambhava is brought into the central courtyard of Kathok Monastery and the dance of the dakas is performed. The founder of the Tantric form of Buddhism in Tibet in the eighth century, Padmasambhava came to be venerated as the second Buddha and was referred to as Guru Rinpoche, or "precious teacher." Owing to his capacity to adapt to myriad circumstances, he was credited with varied manifestations and is often represented with a retinue of dakas and dakinis—the male and female energies that bring all things to fruition. The dakas' ritual hand drums are made of inverted skulls, the sound of which subdues conceptual thought, revealing deeper levels of awareness.

THE WAY OF THE WARRIOR

At the height of summer the grasslands of Tibet are blanketed with gentian, edelweiss, and other delicate alpine flowers. Villagers and nomads from surrounding districts gather on the flower-carpeted plains and set up great white canvas tents and pavilions decorated with appliqué symbols of good luck and prosperity. The nomads, their faces darkened by the sun, come with dried meat, yak cheese, butter, medicinal herbs, sheepskins, and the pelts of wolves, leopards, and Tibetan foxes. Villagers bring agricultural produce, local silver-work, wooden saddles, or items of trade from China—bricks of tea, silk brocade, cooking pots, and small mirrors. But most importantly they come with horses.

The week-long summer festivals preserve some of the most ancient customs of Tibet. Often traveling great distances, families gather on communal land to venerate the indigenous tutelary gods dwelling on the high ridges and surrounding mountains and to pay homage to the lords of the soil with dances, dramas, archery contests, and feats of horsemanship.

Tales of magical horses and supernatural equestrian feats pervade Tibetan history, from the origin myths of the pre-Buddhist Bon religion to the legend of the great king Trisongdetson, who was killed by a stray arrow while viewing a horse race in Lhasa. Prayer flags, ubiquitous in Tibet, are most commonly emblazoned with a wind horse, or *lungta*—a symbol of strength and vitality carrying one's dreams and aspirations to the celestial spheres. Most resonant, however, is the legacy of Gesar of Ling, who with his winged horse inspires oracles and bards, kings, lamas, and warriors alike with his code of spiritual warriorship.

As a young child, Gesar, the legendary Tibetan hero sent by the gods to restore order on the earth, was exiled from the land of Ling by his ambitious paternal uncle Kotong. With great fanfare and overarching confidence in his anticipated victory, Kotong challenged the chieftains of the surrounding lands to a horse race. The winner would inherit the ancestral treasures, rule over all the land, and receive as his queen the beautiful Dugmo—a dakini in human form promised at birth to Gesar, the rightful heir. Riding a wild, celestial horse that only Dugmo could have captured and tamed, Gesar returned from exile, won the race, and was proclaimed divine ruler of Ling—a region of present-day Kham in eastern Tibet.

On the high plains between Paiyul and Nyarong, Khampa men, their long robes trimmed with tiger, leopard, and otter skin and silver-sheathed swords slung through their belts, prepare their horses for the competition. Rearing on their hind legs, the horses are feisty, almost jittery, in contrast to their riders, who nonchalantly rehearse the acrobatic stunts that will edify the ancestral gods and ensure the admiring glances of the Khampa maidens. These young women are already touring the fields in small groups; the coral, turquoise, and amber stones braided into their hair indicate that they are still single. Parents sit on thick carpets inside their open tents, serving meat, tea, tsampa, and chang to new and old acquaintances, playing board games, and speculating on prospective romances and marriages.

Sons and daughters of the freedom fighters who fought ruthlessly against invading Chinese forces, the Khampas of today are no less imposing. In loose flowing pants, shirts of raw silk, and high leather boots, the riders gather at the end of the field. Perhaps a thousand spectators form two parallel rows, each about three hundred meters long, between which the horsemen now gallop, crying out to the gods as they arch back off their saddles, and, their hands nearly trailing the ground, scoop up the white ceremonial scarves placed along the course. At full gallop, each rider in succession performs a series of acrobatic maneuvers, demanding unwavering confidence. Their graceful movements make Western rodeos seem crude feats of endurance at best. Then, still astride their charging steeds, the riders shoot at targets with arrows and rifles, sometimes aiming with one hand from beneath the racing horse. "Between events," says Rapten Dorje, a Khampa freedom fighter now living in Nepal, "the riders swagger about the edges of the field, feigning indifference to the admiring glances of the women."

In ancient times Tibet's horsemanship was legendary throughout central Asia, its warriors feared and admired. Far from a rigid militancy, the Tibetan martial spirit exults in risk taking, in exceeding established limits. In Tibet's pre-Buddhist shamanistic tradition, horses were associated with transcendence—the journey to other spheres. Bon priests "rode" their drums while Tantric yogins and yoginis travel figuratively on the backs of tigers, snow lions, and celestial horses. On the earthly plane accomplished horsemanship signifies the power and unbridled vitality of the tribe. In the

Dunhuang chronicles it was the king's steed that subdued the four frontiers. For the descendants of Gesar—the warrior king—horsemanship conveys a sense of self-mastery and leads the rider to surrender fearlessly to a higher force. "The purpose of warriorship," explains Trungpa Rinpoche, a direct heir of Gesar of Ling, "is to conquer the enemy . . . of our cowardly minds and uncover our basic goodness, our primordial confidence. . . . It is the very opposite of defensiveness, struggle, or aggression."

THE WAY OF SURRENDER

Tibetans believe the mark of the true warrior is less his prowess in battle than his courage to surrender self-concern to a higher principle or cause. In the chivalry of the Christian Middle Ages, a knight's egotism and aggression were tempered through platonic love and devotion to his lady. The Tibetan code of warriorship is less ethereal and inhibited. Rosy-cheeked Khampa women, bedecked in fur-trimmed brocades and rich ornaments of silver, turquoise, amber, and coral, feign shyness but are at heart as bold as their male counterparts. With a flashing smile, subtle eye gesture, or resolute turn of the head, a romance can be initiated, arranged, or resignedly abandoned.

As night falls, bonfires blaze under a vast starry sky, and almost until dawn nomads and villagers perform regional dances in honor of the local gods, accompanied by men and women singing alternating verses of ancient folk songs. Chang—Tibetan barley beer—is consumed in great quantities after the first drops have been flicked in the four directions as offerings to the attending spirits of the land. Although put out to pasture for the night, horses often reappear in the lyrics of Tibetan ballads. As one Khampa sings: "When I ride a horse I hold my seat. When I play with dangerous maidens I let them talk first." Other songs focus on the fleeting nature of life's pleasures, the transience of men's wealth and women's beauty, and the vagaries of summer weather.

THE DANCE OF IMPERMANENCE

In summer, monsoon clouds often rise over the crest of the Himalayas, bringing rain, hail, and sometimes snow to the high Tibetan plateau. Downpours alternate with periods of intense sunlight; the shifting weather turns the summer landscape into a

continual drama of darkness and light. Tibetans learn from an early age to adapt to fluctuating conditions and, instead of resisting change, to rejoice in the renewal that changing seasons and circumstances bring. On the final day of the summer festival, amid the packing up of tents and stores, promises are made to meet the following year, and romances or love affairs are tenderly suspended.

Stormclouds billowing over the granite peaks to the east contrast with the brilliant sunshine that casts an ephemeral golden light on the emptying fields. A double rainbow arches over distant

With ceremonial drums held aloft, monks descend the Potala Palace staircase on their way to the Monlam Torgyak ceremony of the New Year's festival.

hills already veiled in rain. A lone Khampa girl in otter-trimmed brocades walks her dappled horse across the illuminated grass, glistening now in the first drops of the advancing rain. In a few months these grassy plains will be covered in snow and ice, and twelve months from now they will again resound with ancestral songs and the thunder of horses' hooves. Caught in the luminous drizzle and ethereal light of the setting sun, the distant tents and small silhouetted figures bustling around them appear as if suspended in time, absorbed in a way of life full of vitality and joy, rooted not only in their own past but somehow representing a common ancestry from which we have strayed but immediately recognize as familiar.

At Khathok Monastery, too, midway through the ceremonial dances, it began to rain. As the sky darkened and the first drops fell, the crowd shifted to find shelter under overhanging roofs. Two figures dressed as skeletons emerged from the monastery and in an intricate interweaving dance circled the outer edges of the courtyard, confronting spectators with their unsettling appearance. These lords of the charnel grounds, eerily synchronized with the shift in weather, remind the celebratory crowd of the fleeting nature of all composite things. To simple pilgrims the dancing specters are humbling

admonishments to accumulate as many good deeds as possible in the hope of a better future life and final release from the wheel of cyclic existence. For the more reflective observer they represent the play of impermanence, a reminder that for our revels to have meaning they must be undertaken not in a spirit of forgetfulness but in full awareness of the actuality of death and rebirth.

At their subtlest the dancing skeletons represent the moment-to-moment processes of birth and death occurring ceaselessly within and around us. From the point of view of Tibetan Tantrism, the charnel ground is not a final terminus but a place of passage pregnant with possibility. Yama, the Tibetan Lord of Death, who holds in his outstretched arms the Wheel of Life, has no objective existence but manifests through our projections and states of inner contraction. From a Tantric point of view the Lord of Death is also the bestower of life liberated from fears, rigid attitudes, and fixed beliefs. Unlike the Grim Reaper, who heralds the loss of all that is precious, the skeleton dancers—lords of the charnel grounds—represent less cessation than celebration of the unending flow of change and transformation that animates all existence and from the seeds of dissolution conceives anew.

During the final days of the Monlam Festival, archery, shooting contests, and horse races were held on the Trapchi plains on the outskirts of Lhasa. It also was customary for the cavalry to pass in review.

At the Paiyul summer festival in eastern Tibet, Khampa horsemen charge down the field at full gallop. "A wise man and a swift horse make themselves famous when they are displayed outside; a woman and an antique turquoise are honoured when hidden at home."
—Ancient Tibetan proverb

Horseman reaching for a prayer scarf. "When you ride a horse, balance comes not from freezing your legs to the saddle but from learning to float with the movement of the horse as you ride. Each step is a dance, the rider's dance as well as the dance of the horse."
—CHÖGYAM TRUNGPA RINPOCHE

"Gesar's winged horse symbolizes the supreme confidence of the warrior. He is the ideal image of something beautiful, romantic, energetic, and wild that the warrior can actually capture and ride."
—CHÖGYAM TRUNGPA RINPOCHE

During the week-long summer festival at Chongra in the Derge district of eastern Tibet, families gather from surrounding villages and districts. They stay in great tents replete with hand-woven carpets and hanging scroll paintings. Amid the feasting, gambling, and general revelry, dance dramas analogous to the mystery plays of medieval Europe take center stage.

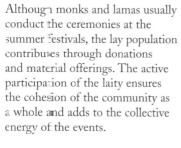

Although monks and lamas usually conduct the ceremonies at the summer festivals, the lay population contributes through donations and material offerings. The active participation of the laity ensures the cohesion of the community as a whole and adds to the collective energy of the events.

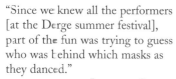

"Since we knew all the performers [at the Derge summer festival], part of the fun was trying to guess who was behind which masks as they danced."
—JAMYANG SAKYA

The *dekar*, or narrator, of the ache lhamo dance dramas recounts historical epics and the lives of the Buddhist saints. Part oracle, part clown, the dekar is also a conjurer, bringing unseen worlds vividly to life.

The *Shepa Tanchen* (dances of joy) unique to the Derge district of Kham,
are performed by lay men and women at times of celebration and rejoicing.
The long sleeves of the dancers signify opulence and bounty.

In the Cham dances spectators see either the reenactment of sacred historical events or the continual transformation of volatile psychic forces. In Tantric Buddhism these shadow energies are not suppressed or rejected but turned to the service of wisdom and compassion.

OPPOSITE
Lords of the Charnel Grounds, thangka painting. Surrendering fearlessly to the inevitability of death, we discover, paradoxically, an open dimension in which birth and death are taking place around us all the time. Vividly dramatizing the unceasing display of life and death, the lords of the charnel grounds symbolize not impending oblivion but the deathless nature of our innermost being. Stripped of the impediments of the flesh, the dancing, grinning skeletons celebrate our naked, imperishable essence liberated from all attachments and obstructions.

TRAGEDY

OMENS AND PROPHECIES

During the Great Prayer Festival in 1933, several months before his death, the Thirteenth Dalai Lama—the living incarnation of Chenresrig, Tibet's patron deity—prophesied the impending destruction of the Tibetan state: "In my lifetime conditions will be as they are now, peaceful and quiet. But the future holds darkness and misery. Religion and government will be attacked from without and within. . . . Monks and government will be destroyed. . . . Lands and properties will be seized. . . . People will be forced to serve their enemies or wander the country like beggars. All beings will be sunk in great hardship and overwhelming fear. The days and nights will drag on slowly in suffering. Such an era will surely come."

In the years preceding his death the Thirteenth Dalai Lama, as Tibet's spiritual and temporal leader, made sustained efforts to formalize the country's independent status, build up its military strength, and increase contact with the outside world. His attempts to end Tibet's policy of isolation were met, however, by strong resistance from a conservative monastic community that feared foreign influence would diminish their own political and spiritual authority. To counter the growing threat of Chinese nationalist and communist incursions and secure its independence, Tibet relied almost exclusively on the power of elaborate religious rites, a strategy

The Thirteenth Dalai Lama seated on the Lion Throne, c. 1930. "The future of our country lies in your hands. Whether you are a chief minister or a simple government official, monk or lay person, teacher or disciple, secular leader or ordinary citizen, I urge you all to rise up together and work for the common good in accordance with your individual capacity. One person alone cannot ward off the threat that faces us; but together we will ultimately prevail."
—LAST TESTAMENT OF THE THIRTEENTH DALAI LAMA

that the current Dalai Lama—the fourteenth in a line of divine incarnations—now suggests was "sentimental" and unrealistic.

Apart from external threats, the period following the passing of the great Thirteenth Dalai Lama and the investiture of the Fourteenth in 1950 was fraught with power struggles within Tibet's monastic and administrative institutions. An attempted coup in 1948 instigated by the Reting regent—the deposed mentor and spiritual preceptor of the young Dalai Lama—led to treachery and discord within the centers of religious and temporal power. Wildly ambitious, the Reting regent invited the Chinese to supply troops and arms, and helped pave the way for the communist invasion two years later. As Tibetan historian K. Dhondrup wrote, "It was one of the darkest periods of Tibetan history, when corruption at every level was rampant and an undercurrent of tension and rapid deterioration in social and moral standards was gradually sweeping across Lhasa."

Several years earlier the State Oracle of Tibet had predicted that 1950—the Year of the Iron Tiger—would be perilous for the country, and indeed, as Radio Beijing proclaimed the impending "liberation" of Tibet, rare astronomical events, devastating earthquakes, and ominous skies suggested to Tibetans the imminence of violent conflict. Further portents included water pouring from one of the golden gargoyles on the roof of the Jokhang—Tibet's most sacred temple—and the inexplicable collapse of a thousand-year-old pillar that had been erected to seal the peace between China and Tibet forever.

The religious ceremonies of 1950 surpassed all earlier displays, as Tibetans mobilized ritual forces at their command to offset the impending peril. Oracles were consulted to determine

ABOVE
The Thirteenth Dalai Lama (seated, fourth from left) with his retinue and British political officer Sir Charles Bell, Darjeeling, India, 1911. When Chinese troops invaded Lhasa in 1910, the Thirteenth Dalai Lama sought refuge in British India. Foreshadowing the communist invasion forty years later, the Dalai Lama told Sir Charles: "I have come to India to ask help of the British government. Unless they intervene the Chinese will occupy Tibet, destroy our religion and political system, and rule the country through Chinese officials."

RIGHT
Government officials seeking prophecies of the future from the Nechung State Oracle.

strategy, but with a disunited military force of only eight thousand troops, the Tibetans proved no match for the invading People's Liberation Army.

INVASION AND OCCUPATION

On October 7, 1950—nearly two decades after the Thirteenth Dalai Lama's Last Testament—the Chinese communist forces entered Tibet, claiming to be "liberating" the country from serfdom and repressive theocratic rule. The newly founded People's Republic of China was lured to Tibet, or, as the Chinese call it, Xizang—"the Western Treasure House"—by the prospects of vast natural resources and strategic terrain in which to carry out its expansionist ideals. In 1951, the year following the invasion, China imposed a Seventeen-Point Agreement for the Peaceful Liberation of Tibet, granting China military suzerainty while ostensibly guaranteeing the protection of Tibet's religious and cultural traditions. Despite widespread international sympathy, neither the United Nations nor any government supported Tibet's quest for independence.

Brandishing pictures of Mao Zedong and Zhou Enlai, twenty thousand bedraggled Chinese marched into Lhasa, and within twenty-four hours the pressure on land and resources began to cause massive inflation and severe food shortages. Welcoming Tibet back to the "Motherland," the Chinese maintained that they had come not to harm but to benefit the Tibetan people. Street songs from Lhasa in the mid-1950s, however, tell another story:

The liberation army has arrived
The herd of beggars has arrived
Everyone has been liberated
Everyone has been made beggars

Not only did the Chinese bring widespread famine and unprecedented taxation, but they also consistently violated the terms of the Seventeen-Point Agreement. Beginning in Tibet's eastern provinces the invaders imposed a series of social "reforms," in the name of which thousands of Tibetans were tortured, killed, or imprisoned, monasteries were destroyed, and land was confiscated and collectivized. Despite the Dalai Lama's visit to Beijing in 1956 to meet with Mao Zedong and discuss China's policy toward Tibet, conditions worsened and large regions of the country remained in a constant state of guerrilla warfare.

Finally, on March 10, 1959, open resistance to Chinese occupation spread to Lhasa. The Tibetan government joined with popular leaders in an uprising against Chinese rule. The Dalai Lama, urged by the State Oracle and hoping to avert a violent confrontation

The Fourteenth Dalai Lama and the Panchen Lama, flanked by Chu Te and Zhou Enlai, arriving at the Beijing railway station, 1954. "Two days later I met Mao-Tsetung for the first time. Mao began by saying he was glad Tibet had come back to the Motherland and that I had agreed to take part in the National Assembly. He said it was the mission of China to bring progress to Tibet by developing its natural resources, and that the generals who were in Lhasa . . . were there as representatives of China to help me and the people of Tibet. They had not gone there to exercise any kind of authority over the Tibetan government or people."
—TENZIN GYATSO,
THE FOURTEENTH DALAI LAMA

After a Tibetan uprising in 1959 to protest
some eight years of Chinese occupation and
oppression, Chinese troops retaliated in brutal
fashion, killing over 87,000 Tibetans in central
Tibet alone. His Holiness the Dalai Lama
and more than 80,000 Tibetans, led by Khampa
guerrilla fighters, fled into exile.

A lama leads the funeral procession of General
Gompo Tashi Angdrugtsang, field commander of
the Tibetan resistance movement, Darjeeling,
India, 1964. "May the tragedy of Tibet be a
warning and a lesson to all mankind and impel
people everywhere to resist tyranny and the
suppression of human rights. May Lord Buddha
bless my country and raise a new Tibet. And
may his noblest representative on earth, the Dalai
Lama, lead our people once again to freedom,
peace, and happiness.
—GOMPO TASHI ANGDRUGTSANG, 1962

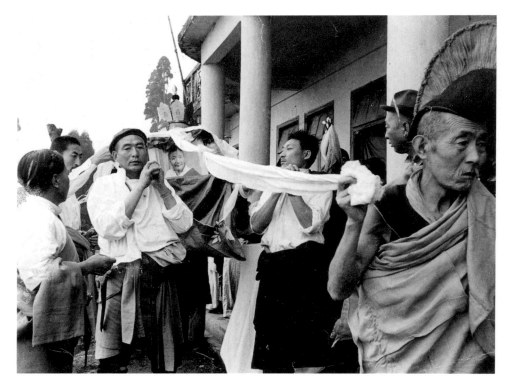

between the unarmed Tibetans and the Chinese army, slipped out of the Norbu Linka Palace disguised as a common foot soldier and, escorted by Khampa resistance fighters, escaped to India. In the ensuing reprisal more than eighty-seven thousand Tibetans were killed and twenty-five thousand imprisoned. More than one hundred thousand, however, followed the Dalai Lama across the Himalayas and into exile.

OPPRESSION AND EXILE

While the Tibetan government-in-exile established itself in the foothills of the Himalayas in northwestern India, conditions in Tibet continued to deteriorate. After 1959 Tibet came under China's direct administration and by 1965 it had been restructured as the Tibetan Autonomous Region, with two-thirds of its original territory absorbed into the Chinese provinces of Chinghai, Gansu, Szechuan, and Yunnan. During the Great Proletarian Cultural Revolution, which swept across China from 1966 until the mid-1970s, waging war on the "Four Olds"—old ideas, old culture, old customs, and old habits—Tibet endured incalculable horrors. Like a grim materialization of the Buddhist hells, more than one million Tibetans—20 percent of the entire population—died as a direct result of Chinese occupation. As reported by refugees, thousands of monks and nuns were crucified, vivisected, burned, buried alive, or had their tongues pulled out with meat hooks for expressing faith in the Dalai Lama. Men and women were publicly tortured to death, nails driven into their eyes and foreheads, or driven to suicide to escape the horror and humiliation. As the International Commission of Jurists Legal Inquiry Committee reported: "It would seem difficult to recall a case in which ruthless suppression of man's essential dignity had been more systematically . . . carried out."

Heeding ancient prophecies, many Tibetans sought refuge in "hidden lands"—idyllic sanctuaries in the Tibetan borderlands revealed by the eighth-century Tibetan saint Padmasambhava. Those seekers who failed to discover these mystical valleys continued through the Himalayas with thousands of other refugees to resettlement camps in India, Nepal, Sikkim, and Bhutan.

In exile Tibetan refugees reestablished their religious and cultural traditions and with international assistance developed such traditional crafts as carpet weaving into highly successful enterprises. In

General Baba Yeshi, once commander of the Tibetan National Volunteer Defence Army in exile in Nepal, standing in front of portraits of himself and Gompo Tashi Angdrugtsang, 1992. Now a monk, Baba Yeshi traveled to Dharamsala in 1991 to visit the Dalai Lama. Greeting him warmly, His Holiness exclaimed: "How extraordinary to receive my general in the robes of a monk!"

Dharamsala, India, the seat of the Dalai Lama's government-in-exile, the Library of Tibetan Works and Archives, the Tibetan Institute of Performing Arts, the Tibetan Medical Center, and numerous schools of philosophy and Buddhist training continue to draw scholars and researchers from around the world.

Despite reforms in Chinese policy under the administration of Deng Xiao Ping and the restoration of previously banned religious and cultural freedoms, resentment of Chinese occupation remains undiminished. Since 1987 there have been numerous demonstrations —often initiated by members of the monastic community—calling for an independent Tibet. Chinese response has been savage, resulting in hundreds of deaths and imprisonments and a new wave of refugees streaming into Dharamsala. In 1989, following massive demonstrations in Lhasa, martial law was declared for more than a year while the Chinese carried out brutal reprisals, including public executions of the "imperialist dogs" who had sought to split the

"Motherland." To this day there are more than ten thousand Chinese troops stationed in Lhasa alone, one for every five Tibetan residents.

China continues to plunder and exploit Tibet's natural resources, clear-cutting forests and dumping nuclear waste. The modernizations that have been made—schools, hospitals, and new employment opportunities—have primarily benefited the Chinese lured to Tibet by attractive economic incentives, including wages that are often more than double the amount they would be earning in China proper. Preferences given to Chinese immigrants have resulted in marginalization and widespread unemployment among native Tibetans throughout Tibet.

The massive influx of Chinese settlers is the newest threat to Tibetan culture and identity. Tibetans have already become a minority in their own country. In what the Dalai Lama refers to as "demographic aggression," the current Chinese policy of "sinofication" and population transfer undermines the cause of Tibetan self-determination and threatens to exile Tibetans within their own land. The six million Tibetans in the Tibetan Autonomous Region and the traditional Tibetan provinces of Kham and Amdo are now outnumbered by seven and a half million Chinese settlers. In Lhasa alone Tibetans are outnumbered three to one. On receipt of the Nobel Prize for Peace in 1989, the Dalai Lama commented: "Tibetans today are facing the real possibility of elimination as a people and a nation. The government of the People's Republic of China is practicing a form of genocide by relocating millions of Chinese settlers into Tibet. I ask that this massive population transfer be stopped."

LEFT

A monk sitting in front of Hindi film posters, Bodhgaya, India. For many Tibetan refugees, dislocation from their homeland is unrelievedly painful. Although most of the 110,000 Tibetans living in exile escaped Tibet following the 1959 uprising, since 1987 an estimated one thousand new refugees slip across the borders to safety and religious freedom each year, only to encounter the difficulties of adjusting to a new life in an unfamiliar land.

BELOW

Tibetan self-help refugee center, Darjeeling, India. "I feel that the Buddhist emphasis on love and patience has helped us considerably in coming through this difficult period of our history. It has helped us to maintain a sense of clarity, strength, and humor. Although almost a quarter of our population was killed, the Tibetan people can still smile and laugh. They can still look to the future with eyes of hope. We call it *Sem-zangpo*, 'the good heart.' We have been treated very brutally. Many have died, many others have spent years in concentration camps under inhuman conditions. But as a people we still possess 'the good heart.'"
—TENZIN GYATSO, THE FOURTEENTH DALAI LAMA

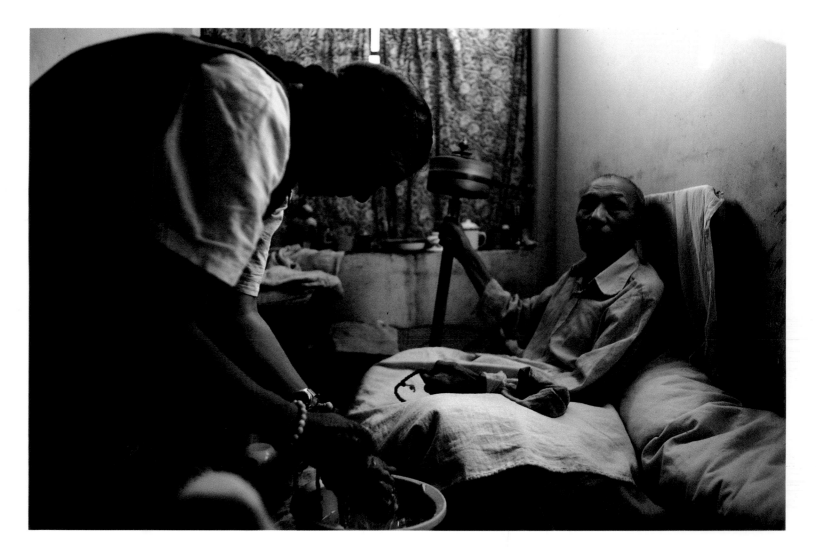

Topai Adhi caring for her aged brother, a monk, Dharamsala, India. Adhi escaped from Tibet in 1991, having survived more than thirty years of brutal persecution and imprisonment because of her husband's involvement with the Tibetan resistance movement. She will never forget the day in 1959 when the Chinese came for her: "Six policemen came to arrest me. My three-year-old son and one-year-old daughter were both with me. As they tied me up with ropes, the baby lay innocently on the bed, but my little boy kept calling my name and trying to come to me. Every time he got near, the policemen kicked and shoved him out of the way. Then when they began to take me away, he fought even harder to reach me, but the police kicked him viciously. I could hear him screaming from a long way off. I wish I had died that day. It was the worst day of my life." Adhi was first taken to Kanze prison in eastern Tibet for interrogation. Sentenced to sixteen years for anticommunist activities, she was then taken to another prison—a gutted and converted monastery—and, like other female prisoners, was repeatedly raped. In 1974, her prison term complete, Adhi was transferred to a labor camp where she was designated a political outcast and forbidden to communicate with people or even raise her eyes from the ground. Working long hours at a brick factory, "I was looked down on and bullied by everyone," she says. In 1979 her "black-hat" status was at last removed and she was sent to a construction site, relieved that "at least we didn't have Chinese holding guns at our backs, and we did receive a little pay."

Palden, a bread maker from Amdo province, now living in Dharamsala, India. "The Chinese killed my whole family. I joined the guerrillas when I was fourteen and later escorted His Holiness out of Tibet and continued to fight the Chinese until the early 1970s. Now I'm just a bread maker. But by the grace of His Holiness I am alive. I pray that some day our country will be free and that I may be able to die in my native land."

A Buddhist fresco, defaced by Chinese troops, Phuntsoling Monastery, central Tibet.

STUDENT: What caused the war between the Chinese and the Buddhists?
TRUNGPA RINPOCHE: Well, the Communists don't like meditation practice. They think it is a waste of time. They think that people should be working all the time. Meditation produces too much personal strength. The communists want to produce group strength, not personal strength. They do not believe in the basic goodness of the group. That's why it is called communism; that's it in a nutshell.

During the Cultural Revolution all but eleven of Tibet's six thousand monasteries were destroyed. Founded in the fourteenth century beside the Tsangpo River in central Tibet, Phuntsoling Monastery once housed over three thousand monks. Now it is in ruins. "We were forced to dynamite the monastery and take it apart brick by brick. They brought in the PLA (People's Liberation Army) to supervise us. I was just a young boy, but I remember the monks weeping. One monk tried to stop us and was shot."
—DAWA PELGYE,
PHUNTSOLING VILLAGER
(Photograph by Thomas Laird)

The Jonang Kumbum, in the remote
Phuntsoling Valley, once housed
thousands of sacred images symbolizing
the totality of the Buddha's teachings.
Blasted by dynamite in 1959, this
once magnificent temple is still eerily
imposing. Chips of fourteenth-century
mural paintings and beheaded Buddhas
litter the ground.

Stripped of his monk's robes thirty years ago, this old, toothless lama in
patched socks and soiled chuba hobbles up the rocky trail every day to prostrate
around the rubble of the Jonang Kumbum, which in its earlier glory was known
as Tongdrol Chenpo—the great chorten that liberates upon seeing.

After this monastery was destroyed during the Cultural Revolution, it was used as a stable. The Chinese treated Tibetan monks no less cruelly, as a lama from Chamdo recalls: "We were brutally beaten and forced to kneel on broken glass with our bare knees. Then many of us were thrown on our backs on the ground and our arms and legs were pulled apart. The torture also included tearing off the prisoner's ears and nose from his head. Some prisoners were blinded when the Chinese poked their fingers into their eye sockets and extracted their eyeballs. Others had dirt stuffed into their mouths, causing them to choke and suffocate. Then they would laugh in our faces and say, 'Now where is your God? If he exists, call him.'"

FREEDOM FIGHTERS

As recent riots and pro-independence demonstrations in Tibet indicate, Tibetans—particularly ordained monks and nuns—actively continue to oppose Chinese occupation and the suppression of Tibetan religion. In addition to a longstanding tradition of militant monks in some of Tibet's largest monasteries, resistance to Chinese domination began in Tibet's eastern frontiers under the leadership of fierce Khampa warriors known for their spirit of independence and utter fearlessness in battle. Several Khampa women—such as Drebo Tayang and Chime Dolma—left their families to lead bands of guerrillas in defiance of Chinese incursions into their homeland. In 1957 tribal chieftains from the mountainous provinces of Amdo and Kham formed an alliance called Chushi Gangdruk, or Four Rivers Six Ranges, establishing a united front against the invading Chinese forces. Sabotaging People's Liberation Army (PLA) convoys and installations, the Chushi Gangdruk secured the mountain districts south of Lhasa, making possible the Dalai Lama's escape into exile in 1959. As Tuktup Gompo Bachungpen, a veteran of Chushi Gangdruk, explains: "Since the Chushi Gangdruk used violence in an attempt to preserve religion in Tibet, it was a different type of violence. . . . The Chinese were destroying monasteries and we were trying to prevent them. When you kill a man for his money, that is one thing; but when you do it to defend your religion, that is another."

The United States government, in its own attempts to curb the spread of communism, secretly assisted the Tibetan resistance movement from 1959 to 1971, training Khampas in guerrilla warfare in the Rocky Mountains of Colorado. So secret was the operation that many recruits never knew they were in the United States. After rigorous training, selected members of this group were supplied with weapons, miniature radios, and suicide pills before being airdropped into Tibet to establish resistance cells. Bases were created near the Tibetan border in northern India and Nepal from which Khampas carried out covert missions, destroying road links, conducting espionage, and engaging PLA convoys. But during the Nixon administration, when the United States renewed its relationship with China, the CIA broke off contact with the Tibetan resistance. The Dalai Lama noted sadly that "U.S. assistance had been a reflection of their anti-communist policies rather than genuine support for the restoration of Tibetan independence."

In a guerrilla war committed to preserving Tibet's sacred heritage, many monks and even reincarnate lamas joined the revolt. Although the Bodhisattva vows, central to monastic ordination, pledge adepts to relieving all sentient beings from ignorance and sorrow—and most Tibetans are loath to kill even ants and mosquitoes—the teachings of Tantric Buddhism allow for the taking of life providing more lives will be saved as a result. The Dalai Lama himself commented that although "from the Buddhist point of view violence is generally condemned . . . under certain circumstances when there is no alternative, when compassion and wisdom fail, then violence is permissible." The Khampas themselves are more pragmatic. As Lhasang Tsering, active in Tibet's resistance and now living in exile in Dharamsala, says: "The Dalai Lama is a saint. I am an ordinary being. We are human beings first and Buddhists second. Fighting is not new to us. We have fought before and we will fight again."

Although most Khampa guerrillas brought with them their tribal loyalties and unresolved feuds, there were many who integrated Buddhist precepts into their armed rebellion against the Chinese. A reincarnate lama from Kham explained how he left his monastery to join the fight against the Chinese. "It was not for my own fame or glory; it was because they were enemies of Buddha's doctrine." Sangwa Tulku, an accomplished Tantric

A statue of the Buddha in ruins, Tsaparang, Tibet.

master, instructed his band of warriors in esoteric Buddhist practices. By performing the rite of *powa* at the moment of taking life, the Khampas learned to transfer the *lha*, or consciousness principle, of the enemy directly to the Buddha realms, preserving their Bodhisattva vows while ridding Tibet of forces hostile to Buddhism. When not engaged in active combat the band took refuge in remote mountain valleys, perfecting the inner yogas that would allow them to liberate beings in the act of depriving them of their lives.

Turning all circumstances into an opportunity to practice the Buddhist teachings, many Tibetans used even the experience of torture and solitary confinement to dissolve the boundaries between self and other. As Sangwa Tulku recalls: "When all means were exhausted, and I was taken away powerless by the Chinese, when they were torturing me, by practicing various methods I meditated on patience, and anger toward them did not arise. . . . I prayed that in countless future lives I might be helpful to them. I thought, May they have the means to be liberated from Samsara, the means to realize the ultimate nature of reality."

The mystical proclivities of the Khampa warriors extended into exile, where many have become monks or engage in traditional meditation retreats of three years, three months, and three days to overcome the inner enemies of ignorance, greed, and aggression and cultivate the mind of enlightenment. When the Dalai Lama met in 1991 with Baba Yeshi, ex-commander of the Tibetan resistance forces, he commented: "How extraordinary to see one of my generals in the robes of a monk!" Despite his insistence on nonviolence in his negotiations with the Chinese, the Dalai Lama expresses deep sympathy for the Khampa resistance. As he said to Khampa Tarchin: "Today I can see your face and you can see mine because of the Khampas. I will never forget this. . . . Tibet can never forget what the Khampas have done. Be happy, and tell your friends also that we are happy about what you have done."

A Buddhist nun being interrogated by the Chinese police. In an interview with the *Guardian*, November 8, 1989, one nun described the torture she and others were subjected to: "They threw us into the truck like so many stones, and took us to prison, twisting our arms behind us. They took away our belts and body-searched us. Then they beat us and chained us to the wall. Later they stripped us and used electric prods all over our bodies, several men at a time, on our eyes, mouth, vagina, everywhere. They used those cattle prods as though they were toys, enjoying themselves, especially when they applied them to our private parts. They weren't human beings, they weren't animals, they were machines. They actually laughed and joked among themselves while they were doing these things. 'You're not nuns now,' they told us, 'You're just garbage.' They never called us by our names, but made us answer to names like pig, horse, donkey, and so on. They laid us face down on the ground, and stripped and beat us. Sometimes they would trample our hands with iron-tipped boots. They kicked us in the face and stomach. Buckets full of urine were put on our heads, while the guards roared with laughter as the urine and excrement streamed down our faces and bodies."

EMBRACING THE ENEMY

Our struggle must remain nonviolent and free of hatred. We must seek change through dialogue and trust. It is my heartfelt prayer that Tibet's plight may be resolved in such a manner that once again my country, the Roof of the World, may serve as a sanctuary of peace and a resource of spiritual inspiration at the heart of Asia.

—The Fourteenth Dalai Lama

The Dalai Lama's plea for nonviolence in addressing the plight of Tibet is not mere pacifism but a dynamic policy rooted in the deepest Buddhist teachings. In a recent address entitled "Embracing the Enemy" the Dalai Lama stated: "Our enemies are our most valuable teachers. . . . While our friends can help us in many ways, only our enemies can provide us the challenge we need to develop tolerance, patience, and compassion." In his uniquely Buddhist perspective the Dalai Lama echoes the ancient sage Santideva, who wrote:

Once the enemy, anger, is destroyed
All other enemies flee like robbers. . . .
Thus, like a treasure found in your own house . . .
An enemy should be received with joy
For he is a friend to the Bodhisattva.

Hatred of one's oppressors, the Dalai Lama has shown, only increases human suffering and blinds us to our own shortcomings. Given the Dalai Lama's transcendental disposition, it is perhaps not surprising that he refers to himself as "half Marxist." Marxism's emphasis on working toward the collective good of society and overcoming class boundaries impressed the Dalai Lama on his visit to Beijing in 1956. As he writes in his autobiography: "The more I looked at Marxism, the more I liked it. Here was a system based on equality and justice for everyone, which claimed to be a panacea for all the world's ills."

During the young Dalai Lama's stay in Beijing, Mao told him that "Buddhism was a good religion—the Buddha having cared considerably for the common people." Mao praised the Buddha, the Dalai Lama recounts, for being "anti-caste, anti-corruption, and anti-exploitation."

"Pö Ranzen" (free Tibet), the monk Champa Tenzin shouts during a 1987 riot.

The real tragedy of Tibet—and, indeed, of China as a whole—is that two systems promising to relieve human suffering—one based on changing the economic substructure of society and the other on transforming man's innermost consciousness—were perceived by their adherents as fundamentally opposed and not as potentially complementary. As the Dalai Lama has repeatedly emphasized, neither the exclusively spiritual nor the exclusively materialistic approach can address all issues of human existence.

In his student days Mao wandered extensively through the Chinese countryside. In his memoirs he recounts how he stopped one evening at a Buddhist monastery to ask for a meal. Mao told the monk who received him that he had not come to worship the Buddha but would like some food. The monk replied, "There is no difference between eating and worshiping the Buddha" and invited him in.

Although in theory Marxism and Buddhism hold many compatible ideals, the problem, as always, remains one of implementation. Whereas proponents of Marxism tend to be rigid and authoritarian, many of Tibet's monastic officials, the Dalai Lama concedes, "were Buddhist in name only" and more concerned with the outer trappings of religion than its inner content. "You have to admit," the Dalai Lama says, "that our religion needed purifying. For that, at least, we can be grateful to the Chinese."

However illuminating exile and oppression may be for those with the power to transform experience into impartial awareness, the tragedy of Tibet has yet to prove cathartic. For more than thirty years China's strategic, economic, and political goals in the Land of Snows have led to devastating cultural and environmental losses, and the more recent policy of transferring massive numbers of Chinese civilians into Tibet threatens the very existence of Tibetan heritage and identity.

"Let a hundred flowers bloom, and let a hundred schools of thought contend," wrote Mao Zedong. Yet his visionary socialism quickly devolved into an autocratic, repressive regime unwilling to compromise or even debate. Although the Dalai Lama has often spoken of the compatibility of Marxist and Buddhist thought, he has also stressed that "there is no refuge in ideology." For the Chinese leaders the Dalai Lama is a "wolf in monk's robes" or a "reactionary dog in the hands of the imperialists." For much of the world, however, he represents a union of spirituality and social action as well as a living embodiment of the magic and mystery of Tibet.

"The only way to world peace," the Dalai Lama has said, "is through cultivating inner peace . . . by overcoming the inner enemies of ignorance, anger, attachment, and pride. . . . The Buddhist teachings come down to one point," he adds, "love and kindness. That is the Buddha's message. Not a single word promotes hatred or some kind of holy war." Stressing the importance of universal responsibility and altruistic thought, the Dalai Lama maintains that all beings are interconnected and that "each of us must learn to work not just for our own individual self, family, or nation, but for the benefit of all mankind." Repeatedly the Dalai Lama has pointed out that the fate of Tibet is a global issue and that the loss of Tibet's unique cultural and spiritual heritage will be a 'loss to all humanity. For his attempts to halt human rights abuses in Tibet and his dedication to the path of nonviolence, the Dalai Lama was awarded the Nobel Peace Prize in December 1989. In his acceptance speech the exiled leader of the Tibetan people expressed his conviction that in striving for world peace, "pessimism is our worst enemy. . . . The prize reaffirms our conviction that with truth, courage, and determination as weapons, Tibet will be liberated."

Chinese armored personnel carriers arrive in Lhasa in March 1989 to enforce martial law. "Tibet and China shall abide by the frontiers which they now occupy. All to the east is the country of great China; and all to the west is, without question, the country of great Tibet. Henceforth, on neither side shall there be waging of war nor seizing of territory. . . . Between the two countries no smoke nor dust shall be seen. There shall be no sudden alarms and the very word 'enemy' shall not be spoken. . . . All shall live in peace and share the blessing of happiness for ten thousand years." —from the peace treaty signed in A.D. 821 by the kings of China and Tibet. The words of this treaty were inscribed on obelisks set up outside the Chinese imperial palace in Beijing and the Jokhang Temple in Lhasa.

ABOVE
Soldiers armed with AK-47s patrol
Lhasa during the imposition of martial
law, March 1989.

RIGHT
Two young Tibetan monks run into a
burning police station in an attempt
to free prisoners trapped inside,
October 1, 1987. The riot that began
that day was the first in a series over
the next several years.

Tibetan civilian being arrested by a Chinese police officer during a pro-independence demonstration in 1989. "Reports of torture include the use of electric batons to beat and sexually assault detainees, suspension of prisoners by wrists and ankles, burning the skin with lighted cigarettes, and brutal beatings with iron bars and nail-studded clubs. Several hundred pro-democracy protesters have been arrested in Tibet since 1987; many have been killed and scores of others tortured."

—AMNESTY INTERNATIONAL

PILGRIMAGE

"ABIDING NOWHERE, POSSESSING NOTHING": PILGRIMS AS REFUGEES

Leaving all they had known behind, the Tibetans' journey into exile was paradoxically a pilgrimage to the origins of their Buddhist faith. Descending into the plains and jungles of northern India, the refugees found solace and inspiration in the shrines and holy places connected to the life of the historical Buddha, whose teachings on compassion and impermanence have permeated Tibetan civilization for the past thirteen hundred years. "Had we not been forced to leave our country," states an elderly woman circling the towering shrine in Bodhgaya that marks the site of the Buddha's enlightenment, "I would never have been able to visit this sacred place. . . . I'd still be in Tibet herding yaks." Without pausing to dwell on the painful realities that drove her and more than a hundred thousand other Tibetans into exile, Pema Lhamo continues her circumambulation, her spinning prayer wheel reflecting in miniature her own pious orbit around the temple.

Becoming an ordained Buddhist traditionally meant giving up one's home and possessions and entering a community of mendicants, becoming in essence a pilgrim—or a refugee. As Trungpa Rinpoche explained, "Becoming a refugee is acknowledging . . . that

Sacred mountains on the Tibetan frontier, Mustang, northern Nepal.

I have journeyed to sacred places in utter joy,
Like a swan landing on a lotus lake
And the vase of my heart is filled to the brim with the
Nectar of their sublime qualities.
—THE THIRD KHAMTRUL RINPOCHE

there is really no need for home or land. Taking refuge in the Buddha is an expression of freedom because as refugees we are no longer bound by the need for security."

The Buddha himself exemplified the condition of homelessness by leaving his palace in search of enlightenment. Thousands of Tibetan refugees, forced into following the Buddha's example, and with the courage to see in adversity a hidden significance, have likewise left their homeland in search of new horizons. As the eleventh-century Tibetan sage Jetsun Milarepa proclaimed in one of his "songs of realization," "Just leaving one's homeland is to accomplish half of the Dharma," inferring, perhaps, that our greatest awakenings often occur when we are impelled by circumstances beyond domestic concerns and attachments and urged into a more inclusive world.

Chatral Rinpoche, a lama from eastern Tibet renowned for his freedom from worldly attachments, was once on pilgrimage with several of his disciples. They stopped at the house of a wealthy trader, who offered Chatral Rinpoche a priceless vase from the Ming dynasty. The vase was carefully wrapped and secured in one of the horse's saddlebags. As they continued on, however, much bickering arose among the disciples over who should look after the porcelain vase. Finally, Chatral Rinpoche took the vase out of the bag, held it aloft, and said, "I'll show you who will take care of it," whereupon he broke it over his knee. The priceless porcelain shattered into shards on the ground, revealing the fragility and transience of all that we assume to be valuable and enduring. "From this point on," Chatral Rinpoche stated, "our pilgrimage begins."

For Tibetans, pilgrimage refers to the journey from ignorance to enlightenment, from self-centeredness and materialistic preoccupations to a deep sense of the relativity and interconnectedness of all life. The Tibetan word for pilgrimage, *neykhor*, means "to circle around a sacred space," for the goal of pilgrimage is less to reach a particular destination than to transcend through inspired travel the attachments and habits of inattention that restrict awareness of a larger reality. "In essence," Chatral Rinpoche explains, "We abide nowhere, we possess nothing." On pilgrimage old habitual patterns and routines are given up as resolutely as an encumbering Chinese vase, as so much excess baggage. For the true pilgrim the sense of renunciation—of letting go—is not perceived as loss. Rather, as one lama put it, "What the pilgrim renounces finally is anything in his experience that is a barrier between himself and others."

PLACES OF PASSAGE: THE GEOGRAPHY OF SPIRIT

The intensity of the Tibetan landscape and the demands it exacted from its human residents shaped the consciousness of the Tibetan people long before the arrival of Buddhism. Treacherous, often malevolent spirits ruled over the elements of earth, air, and water, influencing and often undermining the aspirations of their human intercessors. These "lords of the earth" were enjoined for assistance, or their dissonant energies were averted through offerings or sacrifices. Their essential nature, however, remained ambiguous and uncertain, keeping Tibetans in uneasy intimacy with their land. At the founding of the first Buddhist monastery in Tibet in the eighth century, the indigenous spirits were unappeasable and thwarted all attempts at construction. King Trisongdetson sent to India for the powerful Tantric sage Padmasambhava, whose power of insight and awareness subdued Tibet's belligerent deities, converting them into protectors of the Buddhist path to enlightenment. An ancient biography of Padmasambhava quotes him as saying to the king: "Mighty ruler, great king, this country of yours is indeed full of harm-bestowing demons and spirits. While coming here, I bound by oath the gods and demons of the land. . . . Since I understand all dualistic conceptions as nothing other than mind, the terrors caused you by gods and demons in me brings no anxiety. . . . In the essence of mind itself, beyond imagining, there are no gods and neither are there demons."

Padmasambhava's journey through Tibet deepened the Tibetan people's awareness of their environment and of the powers of the human mind to shape reality. By subduing volatile psychic energies and compelling the indigenous shamanistic gods to serve as guardians of the Buddhist path to enlightenment, Padmasambhava changed the Tibetans' relationship to their land from a tenuous alliance to one of resonance and possibility. Places once associated with equivocal spirits became places of pilgrimage and spiritual retreat where primal forces of mind and nature were no longer perceived as threatening but as intimate reflections of one's innermost being. The powerful mountain gods of Tibet, once linked with individual clans and tribes, lost their exclusive affiliations and came to unify Tibetans within a common vision of the sacredness of their land and a recognition that enlightenment could be sought only with an attitude of openness and compassion that takes all beings into its embrace. As Trungpa Rinpoche wrote: "The theistic beliefs that existed in Tibet—the belief in self and god as separate . . . the primitive beliefs in the separate reality of me and my object of worship—all had to be destroyed. Unless these dualistic notions are destroyed, there is no starting point for giving birth to Tantra."

The caves, mountains, and secret grottos where Padmasambhava and the early *siddhas*—or realized ones—of Tibet converted local deities into defenders of the Buddhist faith, developed into hermitages and places of spiritual retreat, where the higher stages of the Buddhist Tantras could be more readily perfected. Temples and shrines constructed at these sites completed their transformation from places associated with malevolent nature spirits to Buddhist sanctuaries. This "taming of the earth foundation," as it is called in Tibetan, unlike the Christian suppression of indigenous pagan practices in Europe, did not destroy the old religion of Tibet but absorbed the power and sacred history already attached to these holy sites, reinterpreting them in light of a doctrine beyond superstition or dualistic vision.

These places of transformation developed immense significance for lay Tibetans who to this day come to make offerings and receive teachings from resident yogins and yoginis and absorb the numinous energies of places where compassion and insight have triumphed over fear and aggression. By traveling to sacred sites Tibetans are brought into living contact with the icons and energies of Tantric Buddhism. The *neys,* or sacred sites themselves, through their geological features and the narratives of transformation attached to them, continually remind pilgrims of the liberating power of the Tantric Buddhist tradition. As Tara Tulku explains, however, it is not merely a shift in belief or symbolism that affects our experience at these sacred places: "The great yogins and yoginis, through their spiritual attainments, their vows, and prayers, created empowered spaces where past, present, and future are all equally accessible." Another lama maintains, "Just going to these places with faith and openness can transform the mind in much the same way that Padmasambhava transformed the deities and spirits that inhabit these sacred sites."

Pilgrimage in Tibet developed within the context of a visionary landscape where power places, or neys, associated with Tantric deities could open the pilgrim to a timeless presence and dispel beliefs in the separateness of the human and the divine. Over time pilgrimage guidebooks were written, giving instructions to pilgrims visiting the holy sites and accounts of their history and significance. These guidebooks, or *neyigs*, empowered Tibet and its people with a sacred geography, a narrated vision of a world ordered and transformed through Buddhist magic and metaphysics. In the context of the pilgrimage sites, the Buddhist deities could be understood ultimately as the mingling of the creative forces of nature and human consciousness, and demons came to be perceived as the dissonant and obsessive forces of greed, fear, and aggression arising from the illusion of a separate self.

SACRED WORLD VIEW: THE HIDDEN LANDS OF PADMASAMBHAVA

The culmination of Tibetan sacred geography is embodied in the "hidden lands," or *beyul,* concealed by Padmasambhava and later revealed by his lineage holders. The notion of an earthly paradise— a Shangri-la—hidden in the recesses of the Himalayas was popularized in James Hilton's novel *Lost Horizon.* The story of Shangri-la borrowed heavily from Tibetan legends of a mythical Buddhist kingdom called Shambhala, believed to exist in another dimension of time somewhere north of Tibet. Less well known is the related Tibetan tradition of beyul—remote sanctuaries hidden behind the ice walls of the Himalayas and imbued with mysterious powers. Beyul serve as places of spiritual awakening where, according to an early pilgrimage guidebook to the hidden land of Pemakö,

"What in other places can be achieved in one year, here can be achieved in one night." If they can be found, beyul also serve as places of refuge during times of war or calamity. "When the time of war, famine, and epidemics begins," continues the same text, "it will be the time to enter the hidden places of Padmasambhava. These are of many kinds—some are safe for years, some for months, some forever."

When the Chinese invaded Tibet, many lamas, following the prophecies contained in these sacred texts, led their disciples—and in some cases entire communities—into the wilderness in search of Padmasambhava's hidden lands. Some lost their way, others were turned back by local guardian deities, and still others, following pure visions, entered waterfalls or other mysterious portals, never to return to this dimension. Beyul exist on three levels—outer, inner, and secret—and while several such places have been opened outwardly and support small communities of spiritual practitioners, their innermost dimensions remain sealed until the time Tibetan prophecies refer to as "The Great War"—an impending apocalypse that can be averted only by a profound shift in human nature.

The earthly paradise for Tibetans is not a paradise lost, but an immanent landscape of planet and psyche alike. The qualities even of the outer beyul can be extraordinary. Sechu Palden, a woman born in the hidden land of Pemakö, describes visions appearing in waterfalls and lakes, and pools of water with miraculous healing qualities. Her family traded in medicinal plants, some of which had the power, she claims, to shift the mind into states of clairvoyance and profound meditation. Birds and animals gave direction, and omens and portents could be read from rocks and trees. The entire landscape, as Sechu Palden describes it, was imbued with supernatural power. "When people die in Pemakö," she maintains, "rainbows appear emanating from their bodies." When I ask, half incredulously, if she herself had witnessed such phenomena, she replies emphatically: "Not just me; everybody sees these things in Pemakö."

The hidden lands have their own local protectors— temperamental beings tamed by Padmasambhava but still as easily offended as appeased. The guidebook to Pemakö warns: "If you aren't careful, the protectors will cause perilous circumstances testing the power of your realization. . . . They will help those who keep their spiritual commitments (*damsig*) and punish those who do not." In the charged atmosphere of a beyul, the cutting of particular trees or the defiling of sacred plants or water sources can have disastrous consequences. When the king of Powo—a region in southern Tibet—went on a pilgrimage to Pemakö with his eldest son, the prince, thinking he was someone special, urinated at the sacred site of Buddhatsepung and was immediately crushed by a boulder—the victim of his own sense of self-importance and an uncompromising environmental ethic.

In any country, wild, uninhabited places have the potential to rouse us from self-centered perceptions and connect us more vitally to the surrounding world. Tulku Pema Wangyal, a lama who spent several years in Pemakö, maintains that in hidden lands, "our own inner elements harmonize with the external elements and we enter into a natural state of meditation. . . . A profound resonance develops between what is inside and what is outside. . . . At the innermost level the hidden land serves as a means of recognizing that at heart there is no distinction between ourselves and the world around us."

The hidden lands of Padmasambhava are ultimate places of pilgrimage, revealing a world transformed through sacred vision. "Even the snakes here," says a pilgrim returning from Pemakö, "aren't to be seen as just dangerous; they are supports for our mindfulness." Khamtrul Rinpoche, a visionary lama living in Dharamsala, proclaims: "All regions of the earth have their own secret places," and whether we visit them in person or only in mind, through them our experiences of the phenomenal world can be intrinsically transformed. As Trungpa Rinpoche wrote, "If we open our eyes, if we open our minds, if we open our hearts, we will find that this world is a magical place." Seeing not only with the eyes but with the heart, we expand our sense of belonging to all creation, to all life. And true pilgrimage, though it may take us to the far corners of the earth, always begins and ends in the heart.

Chortens near Samye Monastery, Utsang, central Tibet. Carved out of living rock, five white chortens revered as the five transcendental Buddhas mark the site where the Tibetan emperor Trisongdetson met Padmasambhava in the year 765. Joining earth and sky the stupa symbolizes the path to liberation from cyclic existence. It also represents Tibetan Buddhist and Bon cosmology, in particular the metaphysical Mount Meru around which the entire universe spins and takes shape. (Photograph by Thomas Laird)

On the pilgrim's circuit around Kang Rinpoche
(Mount Kailas).

A magic spell, a dream, a gleam before the eyes.
A reflection, lightning, an echo, a rainbow,
Moonlight upon water, cloud land, dimness
before the eyes, fog and apparitions,
these are the twelve similes of the phenomenal world.
                                        —NAROPA

Pilgrims and prayer flags on the Dolma-la; at 18,600 feet the highest
point on the pilgrim's circuit around Kang Rinpoche. On pilgrimage the
rigors of the journey are understood to bring both merit and insight.
"With the exception of two old men, all of us decided to walk in order to
increase the merit of our pilgrimage. Our horses and mules would be used
only to carry supplies and merchandise. Emulating the Lord Buddha, we
decided as far as possible to beg for our food throughout the journey."
                                                        —RAPTEN DORJE

A solitary nun circumambulates Kang Rinpoche (Mount Kailas), revered by
Tibetans as the axis of the world. The ancient practice of *parikrama*, or *kora*,
is less one of defining a perimeter than one of dissolving all sense of boundary.
Connecting to the holy site through intimate circumambulations, kora draws
one ever inward toward a sacred center. While Buddhists circumambulate
clockwise, followers of Bon—Tibet's indigenous religious tradition—circle
counterclockwise. When asked why, a Bonpo pilgrim replied, "I'm not following
the Buddha, I'm going to meet him."

Kang Rinpoche (Mount Kailas) and Mapham Yumtso (Lake Manasarovar), viewed from the south. Symbolizing the interpenetration of all phenomena, sacred sites in Tibet are often places where male and female elements in the landscape are joined—a mountain and a lake, for example. Like a mirror, places of pilgrimage reflect back the qualities we see in them.

The famous Mount Kailas
blanketed with snow
symbolizes the pure, white Buddhist
  doctrine.
The streams, flowing into the Blue Lake
  of Mapham
symbolize one's deliverance to the Realm
  of the Absolute.
                              —MILAREPA

Taktsang Hermitage,
Paro Valley, Bhutan.

*In the mountains there is an
    open market
Where the things of this world
Can be bartered for wisdom
    and bliss.
In the monastery of your heart
    and mind
lies a temple where all the
    Buddhas unite.*
                    —MILAREPA

Dorje Drolo—the Manifestation of Crazy Wisdom, thangka painting. Conceived as an ecstatic manifestation of Padmasambhava, the deity Dorje Drolo embodies the forces of insight and compassion beyond logic and convention. Invoking in the practitioner the fearlessness and spontaneity of the awakened state, Dorje Drolo transforms hesitancy and clinging into enlightened activity. He rides a pregnant tigress, which signifies the latent power of our intrinsic Buddha-Nature. Drolo's energy overcomes distinctions of life and death, representing instead a continual process of giving birth to new circumstances and possibilities. Padmasambhava manifested as Dorje Drolo at numerous pilgrimage places in order to subvert indigenous Tibetan belief in demons and malevolent gods, redirecting their powerful energies toward the path of wisdom and compassion.

TRANSFORMATIVE JOURNEYS: THE OUTER PILGRIMAGE

For Tibetans pilgrimage suggests a journey not simply from one place to another but an inner journey—one that through separation from one's habitual routines and preoccupations will bring one closer to the ideals at the heart of Tibetan Buddhist culture. Thus, while the journey may be a personal one, at heart it unites the individual pilgrim with the common values of the larger community.

People engage in pilgrimage for as many reasons as they might turn to religion: curiosity, adventure, worldly profit or disappointment, penance or devotion, or a quest for spiritual fulfillment. Often representing a passage from one stage of life to another, pilgrimage can be a means of purifying misdeeds or unfavorable karma, or seeking circumstances conducive to a higher rebirth. At another level, pilgrimages are made to deepen one's commitment to spiritual practice, to meet with great spiritual masters, to receive empowerments and initiations, and to request esoteric teachings. In essence, however, pilgrimage for Tibetans centers on withdrawing from the petty securities of material life and embracing a reality larger than one's everyday routines.

A nomad family we met in eastern Tibet had recently sold their yaks to collect enough money for the entire family to go on pilgrimage to Lhasa. The journey would take several years, for they would cover the entire distance by prostrating the length of their bodies across the earth, surrendering to the primordial ground from which all Buddhas have arisen. Although they'd been on the road for months their enthusiasm was infectious. After sharing a meal of tsampa and fresh sheep cheese in their tent, we gave the father a photograph of the Jokhang, the holiest shrine in Lhasa. He thanked us profusely, claiming that he was happier than if we'd given him a horse—which for a Tibetan is no small comparison. I reflected as we left their tent that though they would reach "the city of the gods" long after us, it would be a city transfigured and intimately revealed by the faith and passion of their journey.

At a rudimentary level pilgrimages are made to acquire merit—the positive mental and spiritual propensities that will aid one in this life and the next. As one lama explained, pilgrimages are often made because of an inability to recognize the true nature of Buddhist practice, in which the Buddha is not to be found externally but within one's innermost being. Still, for pious pilgrims, holy shrines and the journey toward them have the power to lift one out of one's ordinary, utilitarian concerns. The hardships of the journey—prostrating or walking barefoot or following the example of the Buddha and begging for one's food, sometimes out of necessity—all add to one's store of merit and humility. As Tara Tulku explained: "The more suffering that is undergone on a pilgrimage, the more merit you accrue—provided that the suffering is borne positively. Of course, if you get angry and irritated with your hardships, that will only decrease the merit."

Lamas distinguish deepening levels of pilgrimage. As Tara Tulku explained: "If one goes on pilgrimage just to benefit oneself in this life, it is not considered a religious action, but just an ordinary action, and yet one can still receive some benefit from it. Those of higher aspiration go on pilgrimage not only for the betterment of this life but to achieve liberation and enlightenment. This has a deeper significance. Finally, Bodhisattvas go on pilgrimage for themselves and all other beings simultaneously, dedicating whatever merit accrues for the benefit of all beings."

Tibetans are wanderers, nomads at heart who travel wherever conditions are most favorable for their herds or trade. Much pilgrimage developed in association with long trading expeditions on which merchants would stop off at holy places and offer butter lamps and prayers to ensure safe travel and prosperity in business. Pilgrims often finance their onward journeys by selling animal skins, dried meat, clothing, cooking pots, or even jewelry and heirlooms at pilgrimage centers. In turn they often collect rare medicinal plants at remote sacred places to barter or sell on their return home.

But pilgrims are usually less interested in profiting materially from their travels than in acquiring merit and wisdom through dropping the acquisitive mind. Generosity is one of the six perfections of the Bodhisattva and engenders an inner state conducive to spiritual growth. Offerings—whether of the body through prostrations or the rigors of the journey, or of speech through the recitation of prayers and mantras, or of mind through an attitude of openness and fearless surrender—lead the pilgrim to a recognition that the greatest merit, and the greatest happiness, is achieved through compassion and concern that extend beyond the self.

On pilgrimage—as in life—we travel through myriad realms of existence, an unceasing cycle of self-made heavens and hells. Attentive pilgrims discover that every moment contains the possibility of relinquishing attachments and aversions and attaining a freer, more expansive perspective. Pilgrimage—like meditations on the Wheel of Life—brings us out of ourselves and exposes our essential condition beyond obscuring fantasies and expectations. Through the journey outward our most fundamental attitudes and relationships can be renewed and transformed, preparing us, ultimately, for the inevitable journey home. For as T. S. Eliot wrote, describing a universal human experience, "The end of all our exploring will be to arrive where we started and know the place for the first time." A place made fresh through absences.

"RECEIVING INSTRUCTION FROM ALL THINGS": THE INNER PILGRIMAGE

"It is better to travel well than to arrive," maintains an old Tibetan adage pointing to a still deeper level of pilgrimage. If the outer journey focuses mostly on place and the blessings to be received at particular holy sites, inner pilgrimage focuses more on process. Merit, in this context, is understood less as the number of mantras recited, prostrations performed, or hardships endured, than as the recognition of the unity of mind and phenomenal appearances. As the Buddha himself said, "There is more merit in a single instant of true Awareness than in lifetimes of prostrations or prayers." Each act of awareness has a formative power not just within our own body-mind but on the environment around us. The extraordinary pilgrimage begins with a recognition of the dynamic relationships within all existence—that every moment, every event can be a catalyst for breaking the boundaries of the self and discovering the natural luminosity of our essential condition. As Longchenpa, a fourteenth-century scholar and meditation master pointed out, the sacred places of the extraordinary pilgrimage are not necessarily the same as those visited on ordinary pilgrimages:

> Go to mountain tops, charnel grounds, islets, and fairgrounds . . .
> Places that make the mind waver,
> And let the body dance, the voice sing,
> And the mind project innumerable thoughts:
> Fuse them with the view and meditation of instantaneous
>   self-liberation
> Then all arises as the path.

In the Dzogchen Tantras, the highest teachings in the Tibetan Buddhist tradition, the essence of pilgrimage is embodied in the term *Gang Shar Lam Khyer*—"bringing whatever arises to the path (of enlightenment)." In the nondual perspective of the Dzogchen, or Great Perfection, teachings, path, and goal become one and the same, turning anything encountered into a potential source of spiritual awakening. From this absolute perspective there is nothing either to avoid or especially seek out. Obstacles are viewed less as challenges to be overcome than as opportunities to open and expand. From the point of view of Dzogchen, readiness is all—a fearless state of unbounded empathy.

Linked to the earliest transmission of Tantra in Tibet, Dzogchen teachings called "receiving instructions from all things" urge the pilgrim to abandon attachments to concepts of pure and impure, sacred and profane, and bring forth a mind calm, vast, and playful. As Phadampa Sangye, an early Indian siddha, or realized one, instructed his Tibetan consort-disciple Machig Labdron:

> O daughter, be detached from place . . .
> Approach all that you find repulsive!
> Anything you are attached to let go of it!
> Go to places that scare you, like cemeteries!
> Find the Buddha inside yourself!

From the point of view of Dzogchen, the boundaries between inside and outside dissolve in the all-pervasive interplay of emptiness and luminous appearance. The Tantric injunction to take all appearances as one's consort brings the pilgrim into an intimate relationship with his surroundings, the phenomenal world arising as the magical display of radiant awareness. To extend the old adage, "It is not so much how we travel but how we see." In the esoteric tradition of Tantric Buddhism the eyes and heart are linked by subtle energy channels within the yogin's body. When perception is purified, the heart is simultaneously transformed, opening within us new levels of awareness. William Blake phrased it succinctly, if cryptically, as "the Eye Altering Alters All." The great Indian master Saraha—revered in the Tibetan tradition—similarly proclaimed, "I've seen in my wanderings great shrines and places of pilgrimage, but none are as blissful as my own body."

Following in Saraha's tradition of recognizing the place of ultimate pilgrimage as linked to psychic centers within one's own subtle anatomy, Nyushel Khen Rinpoche, a contemporary Dzogchen master, announced, "Let others travel across the mountains to Bodhgaya....The ultimate place of Buddha's enlightenment is right here on my meditation cushion."

Whether performed internally or externally, pilgrimage is a means of realizing the essence of the Buddhist path of wisdom and compassion. Recognizing the intrinsic purity of all phenomena, the Dzogchen yogin, free of the distinctions of attraction and aversion, perceives the everyday world as a magical sacred realm. The ultimate pilgrim—with compassion as his only compass—he wanders freely, abandoning attachments to property and home, spontaneously liberated in all that he or she encounters. As one realized master proclaimed, "The heart is the hub of all sacred places; go there and roam at will."

Covering several miles a day, monk pilgrims from Kham prostrate the
full length of their bodies along ancient pilgrim routes. Over a thousand
miles remain before they will reach their destination, Lhasa. Generally
considered to be the quickest and most effective way of purifying karma,
prostration is performed at several levels. "Prostration of the body,"
explains one of the monks, "may be anything from folding hands to
a full-length prostration on the ground. Reciting prayers is prostration
of speech. Developing faith and appreciation for the Buddhas and
the qualities they represent is prostration of the mind."

"Prostrating, I can use my whole body to pray," an itinerant monk says. "Many people tell me to meditate or stay in retreat . . . that my sins are all purified, but I prostrate for all beings, not just for myself." Sangwa Rinpoche expands upon this perspective, explaining that on an esoteric level, "prostrations open the body's central channel, preparing it for higher yogic practices."

Prostrating in front of the Jokhang Temple, Lhasa. Housing the image of Lord Buddha brought by Wen Chen Konjo in the seventh century, the Jokhang marks the center of Tibet's sacred realm. One pilgrim recalls his visit: "We did not pause to find lodgings or even drink a cup of hot tea, but headed straight for the Jokhang. There, we paid homage to the Jowo . . . the most sacred image in the whole of Tibet and the source of countless miracles. We offered many butter lamps and prayed long and earnestly."

Pilgrims receiving the Kalachakra Initiation in Sarnath, India. An initiation into the mysteries of esoteric anatomy and cosmic time, or, as the Dalai Lama explains, "the union of immutable bliss and empty form," the Kalachakra empowerment is transmitted to lay practitioners as well as to the monastic community. Unifying the body's inner winds and subtle essences within the central channel, the successful adept gives rise to a state of clarity and bliss, leading ultimately to full enlightenment.

The Fourteenth Dalai Lama conferring the Kalachakra Initiation in Sarnath, India. Because of its profundity, the Kalachakra Initiation can be bestowed only by the most realized of Tibet's lamas. "Rays of light . . . at the heart of the Lama—inseparable from Kalachakra—draw you in. Entering his mouth you pass through the center of his body, and through the vajra path enter the Mother's lotus, melting into a luminous drop which dissolves into Emptiness. From within Emptiness arises a jewel from which you arise as a deity . . . embraced by the consort Mamaki."

—Instructions for visualization in the Kalachakra Tantra

A monk distributes sacred cords blessed by the Dalai Lama at the Kalachakra Initiation in Bodhgaya, India. Pilgrimages are rites of passage from one phase of life to another. The greatest pilgrimages are also initiations into a new order of existence. Traveling vast distances, Tibetans gather at Bodhgaya, the site of the Buddha's enlightenment, to receive the transmission of Kalachakra—initiation into the wheel of time.

Recollecting merely a toenail of the
    Tantric divinities
Who dance over the heads of gods and
    demons alike,
Kalachakra and Consort, the mystical
    lord and lady
Who abide in a mandala palace of vajra
    jewels,
Gives rise to a measureless surge of
    auspicious karma.

—LOBSANG CHOKYI GYALTSEN,
THE FIRST PANCHEN LAMA,
"The Auspicious Song of the
Practice of Kalachakra"

Monks attending the Kalachakra Initiation
at the Mahabodhi Temple in Bodhgaya,
India. The Mahabodhi Temple marks the
site of Buddha's enlightenment twenty-five
hundred years ago. For centuries Tibetans
have made pilgrimages across the
Himalayas to sites connected with the
life of the historical Buddha. From a
Tantric perspective, pilgrimage is more
than paying homage at sacred sites.
Rather, it is believed that the activities
performed at these places become a
memory of the place itself. By attuning
oneself through ritual and meditation to
this timeless presence, similar experiences
can be evoked.

The Potala Palace illuminated by lightning.

Thus shall you think of all this fleeting
* world:*
A star at dawn, a bubble in a stream;
A flash of lightning in a summer cloud,
A flickering lamp, a phantom and a dream.
—THE BUDDHA, "The Diamond Sutra"

"Now I knew the meaning of the saying,
'One who does not get to Lhasa has
only half a human life.' It looked exactly
like the descriptions of it that I had heard
so many times. 'Now I'm really here,'
I thought, 'It's no longer a dream.'"
                    —JAMYANG SAKYA
                (Photograph by Thomas Laird)

Monks prostrating to the stupa at the deer park in Sarnath, India, site
of the Buddha's first teaching. "At Sarnath the Buddha taught the truth
of impermanence; that all things cease and die only to rise again.
He also showed a way beyond this wheel of becoming and dissolution."
—A MONK AT SARNATH

Pilgrims praying by the sacred river in Bodhgaya, India. "Even if we were to die here," says a pilgrim at Bodhgaya, "it would be a great blessing." In many ways pilgrimage is a rehearsal for death, a preparation, in that it involves separation from our old way of life and embracing the unknown. To die in a state of expansion, at the height of life, we die as pilgrims, eager for transformation. "The Buddhist scriptures speak of crossing to the other shore of the river. But you only arrive at the other shore when you realize there is no other shore.... We make a journey to the 'promised land,' the other shore, and we have arrived when we realize that we were there all along. It is very paradoxical."

—CHÖGYAM TRUNGPA RINPOCHE

OVERLEAF
A pilgrim meditating in the deer park at Sarnath, India. All pilgrimage ends with a return to the familiar world that was left behind. Yet if one's journey was successful, the old world has been irrevocably transformed. The end of pilgrimage is to envision a new beginning.

I have visited in my wanderings
shrines and other places of pilgrimage,
but I have not seen another shrine
blissful like my own body.

—SARAHA

OLD AGE

DEATH AND LIBERATION

OLD AGE, SICKNESS, AND DEATH
At Kushinagar in northern India, aged pilgrims, helped along by their relatives, light butter lamps in front of the reclining image of Sakyamuni Buddha. Tibetans maintain that twenty-five hundred years ago the Buddha died here, to teach the world the truth of impermanence and show how life can be illuminated and transformed even in the moment of its passing. I watch the pilgrims in their devotions, one lamp lit from another, one flame brought into being from another—a metaphor in the Buddhist world for the transfer of consciousness from one life to the next—while the Buddha, in eternal repose, shimmers behind rows of gilded butter lamps. Pilgrims come singly or in groups; the young, the old, the healthy, and the infirm, some with canes, some with prayer wheels, to learn from the Great Sage not only the art of living but the art of dying; to recognize it not as an ending but as an essential passage in a continuing cycle or—through realizing our innermost potential—as the gateway into a mystical realm transcending the duality of life and death. The pilgrims circumambulate the old, dilapidated shrine, which marks the end of the Buddha's—and perhaps their own—life journey. Yet as they circle again and again I reflect that for them it is only one life inscribed by innumerable others, each one—the Buddha taught—characterized by the sufferings incurred through resisting change and transformation.

The Wisdom Deity Vajrapani—Revealer of the Tantras, thangka painting. Symbolizing the goal of the highest Tantric practices—the inner unification of our male and female essences—the *yidam,* or meditation deity, Vajrapani helps Tantric practitioners overcome the habitual self-conceptions that keep us spinning on the wheel of life and death.

"The body itself teaches us impermanence....Disease reminds us that life is uncertain, ephemeral," says Tsampa Amchi, a traditional Tibetan doctor. Tsampa has come down from the mountain behind his house, where he was collecting medicinal plants to treat patients at a Tibetan resettlement camp in northern Nepal. "Most of the people here were nomads and traveled great distances with their herds of yak and sheep. They went on long pilgrimages and trading expeditions.... Now some of them can hardly move."

Health in the Tibetan tradition is based on maintaining a vital balance between the body's inner winds and energies—the biological reflections of larger cosmic forces. Medicines derived from precious metals, rocks, trees, resins, animals, and herbs help reestablish lost harmony, but so too can intervention on a psychic or spiritual level. At Tashi Palkhel resettlement camp Lhawa Wangchuk—one of the few remaining Tibetan shamans—treats patients by invoking powerful protector spirits to dispel obstacles to health and well-being. For Wangchuk, whose skills have been validated by the Dalai Lama himself, the art of healing is inseparable from his Buddhist practice. "Some of the spirits that enter me," he says, "were tamed by Padmasambhava. . . . Now they must use their power for the good of all beings." As far as his own power is concerned, Wangchuk takes no credit. As he phrases it, he is simply a vehicle for the gods.

Medicines and shamanic healings can do much to alleviate disease and extend one's life span, but sooner or later, as Tsampa Amchi reminds us, "Death is inevitable." Buddhist texts repeatedly emphasize the impermanence and discontinuity that characterize our entire existence:

What is the use of youth
Which is ultimately destroyed by age?
What is the benefit of health
Which will only end in illness?
What is the good of wisdom in life
If this life lasts not forever?
Aging, sickness, and death follow each other inevitably.

If taken to heart, the Buddha's teachings on impermanence lead not to pessimism or despair, but to a larger, ultimately more selfless, perspective. Only by first recognizing universal sorrow, Tibetans maintain, can we develop the wisdom and compassion that allow us to overcome our personal preoccupations and embrace a more expansive, interconnected reality.

Leaving the shaman's hut at Tashi Palkhel I pass the quarters for the elderly and infirm. An old woman spinning her prayer wheel says: "We are lucky. . . . As the body loses its desires we have more chance to practice Dharma." She laughs at the old man next to her. "When we were young all he could think about was girls and horse riding. Now he puts the same attention into his prayers." The old man smiles toothlessly, delicate hands turning the beads of his rosary, worn smooth with use. "There's more benefit to what I'm doing now in my old age," he says. "Sometimes youth just causes us to go astray."

Throughout life we experience an inevitable and unalterable process of physical change. The body grows, ages, and dies regardless of human will and intervention. Our resistance to this organic process not only gives rise to suffering but alienates us from the very sources of life itself. From a Buddhist perspective the fleeting, ephemeral nature of all worldly phenomena is the natural expression of a dynamic, unbounded universe. Through the practice of the Buddhist teachings, Tibetans maintain, one overcomes the illusion of separation from the full expanse of reality. "If one practices the spiritual path," writes Konchok Tenpai Dronme, "the mind abides in joy, regardless of one's age. Then when death falls one is like a child joyfully returning home."

At the time of death, the body's constituent elements dissolve into each other—earth into water, water into fire, fire into wind. As the wind element dissolves, external breathing stops, and from a Western point of view the person is clinically dead. From the Tantric perspective, however, the moment of death is linked not to inhalation and exhalation, but to the appearance of the Innate Mind of Clear Light. With the dissolution of the coarse levels of consciousness and their supporting winds the white drop inherited at conception from one's father descends from the crown of the head while the red element inherited from one's mother ascends from the navel. Entering the central channel the male and female essences meet at the heart chakra, causing the appearance of the Clear Light of Death. Through the dawning of the Clear Light, those who have achieved stability in meditation recognize the intrinsic nature of their minds and, "like a child jumping into its mother's lap," are liberated into the luminous expanse of Primordial Reality. For most beings, however, unaware of the subtler levels of consciousness, this crucial stage simply passes unnoticed and one enters bardo—a hallucinatory, transitional realm between death and rebirth.

Essentially, the experience of death is no more than a dramatic example of the changes and transitions that occur continuously throughout our lives. As Sogyal Rinpoche writes: "When you really look into the nature of death, it is like a mirror in which the true meaning of life is reflected." According to the Tibetan tradition, rebirth results from the mind's tendency to cling to appearances and grasp dualistically at external phenomena. As this lifetime provides the basis for our experience at death, our state of mind at the time of death, in turn, conditions our next rebirth. To assist in this critical transition, Tibetans—particularly those untrained in meditation—depend upon spiritual masters to guide their consciousness through the intermediary realms to a favorable rebirth. After death, and continuing for a period of up to seven weeks, the disembodied consciousness journeys uncontrollably through a world of visions, prey to its own fears and projections, and constantly imperiled by the possibility of rebirth in nonhuman form.

The rites for the deceased focus on recitations from the *Bardo Thödrol*, the Tibetan Book of the Dead, whose title literally means "liberation through hearing in the Bardo." This sacred text, attributed to Padmasambhava, instructs the dead person, now freed of his body, to direct his consciousness toward final liberation from the cycle of death and rebirth: "The experiences of whiteness, redness, and utter blackness are all the magical display of your own mind. . . . This luminosity of death is Buddha Mind itself. Reset naturally without fabricating or distorting anything . . . in this way you will be liberated into the Dharmakaya—the unbounded expanse of Ultimate Reality."

A pilgrim meditating in front of an image of the Buddha in his final *samadhi*,
a liberated state beyond death or rebirth, Kushinagar, India

This human life, like a butter lamp set out in the wind—
It might last a long time, or it might not.
Not letting ego's hold tighten further
May I truly practice the sublime teachings.
                    —H. H. DUDJOM RINPOCHE,
                       "Heart Essence of the Great Masters"

An old woman in prayer, Datema, northern
Kham.

Where will you go after death?
What will you become? No certainty!
Not having the strength of realized mind
Will death not terrify you?
— THE SEVENTH DALAI LAMA,
        "The Song of Essential Precepts"

An elderly pilgrim feeding pigeons to gain merit, Tsopema, India.

You have obtained this precious human form, so difficult to find.
If you don't make use of it, it will be lost in no time
Only to be eaten by birds and jackals or consumed by fire.
So take advantage of this now and benefit all beings, infinite as the sky.
— KARMA CHAGMEY RINPOCHE,
"Union of Mahamudra and Dzogchen"

Pema Trinley spots her cow poking its head out from under a gate,
Tseruk resettlement camp, Thak Khola, Nepal.

In order to die well, with joy and confidence
Dwelling in the radiance of spiritual awareness . . .
Begin readying yourself now.
—THE SEVENTH DALAI LAMA,
"Meditations on the Ways of Impermanence"

An elderly couple spinning wool, Tseruk
resettlement camp, Thak Khola, Nepal.
"I remember the yaks and the sheep, the
wide open grasslands. . . . The butter and
yogurt were always fresh and pure. . . .
I pray that Tibet will soon be free and that
I can return and die in my homeland."

Tsampa Amchi treating patients, Tseruk resettlement camp, Thak Khola, Nepal. "We're destined to die from the moment we are born," says Tsampa. "As we grow older we shouldn't have too much attachment to our body, but just view it as a lodging which we'll soon be leaving. . . . Isn't it strange how people pray for a long life but are always fearful of aging?"

OPPOSITE
Sonam Tashi and his daughter consulting ancient texts, Kanze, eastern Tibet. A monk earlier in his life, Sonam Tashi was forced to marry during the Cultural Revolution. The few sacred texts he was able to hide from the Chinese he stores in a dilapidated leopard-skin box. The "materialist dreams of the Chinese are unrealizable," he insists. "Ultimately Dharma is our only refuge."

ABOVE
Golok women reciting mantras, Datema, northern Kham. "From time without beginning until this moment you have circled through the six realms, taking one rebirth after another. Birth, old age, sickness, and death have followed each other like beads on a string."
—KARMA CHAGMEY RINPOCHE,
"Taking Death as the Path"

RIGHT
Elderly women going to a monastery to make offerings, Kanze, eastern Tibet.

At the time of death, close friends who have long been together will separate.
Wealth and possessions gained with much effort will be left behind.
Consciousness, like a guest, will leave the guesthouse of the body.
Surrender these worldly comforts in order to practice Dharma thoroughly.
—NYULCHU TOGME ZANGPO,
"The Thirty-Seven Bodhisattva Precepts"

An old man observing his reflection, Tibetan Old People's Home, Rajpur, India.

> *I remember this body when it was a child's*
> *And as it gradually took the form of a youth.*
> *Now its every limb is twisted and worn.*
> *It is my own body, yet it delights not even my own eyes.*
> —THE SEVENTH DALAI LAMA,
> "Meditations on the Ways of Impermanence"

Holding dorje and bell, an aging nun
gazes into a mirror, Swayambhu,
Kathmandu Valley, Nepal. "When
you really look into the nature of
death, it is like a mirror in which the
true meaning of life is reflected. The
changes or small deaths that occur so
frequently in our lives are a living
link with death, prompting us to let
go and revealing the possibility of
seeing, in that gap, the sky-like,
empty, open space of the true nature
of our mind. In the transition
and uncertainty of change lies the
opportunity for awakening."
—SOGYAL RINPOCHE,
"The Mirror of Death"

LEFT
Lhawa Wangchuk, a Tibetan shaman, entering into trance, Tashi Palkhel
resettlement camp, Nepal. The ancient shamanic traditions in Tibet have
not been denigrated or disregarded by Buddhists. Instead, their power has
been assimilated into the view and practice of Tantric Buddhism. Invoking
the transpersonal energies that allow him to separate from his physical
body, Wangchuk invites into his body the healing forces of the Buddhist
gods. Attaining a condition that for most beings is achievable only after
death, Wangchuk dissolves the inner elements and winds that obscure
awareness of a more encompassing reality. He uses his extraordinary
skills for healing and divination. Even more essential, he believes, are the
prayers and meditations that he dedicates to all sentient beings.

CENTER
Wangchuk is possessed by powerful healing deities. The shamanic
trance—dissolving crude levels of consciousness into progressively more
subtle states—simulates the experience of the bardo, the intermediate
realm between this life and the next.

RIGHT
Wangchuk journeying between worlds.

> *When finally your life forces disintegrate,*
> *Watch the elements of the body dissolve,*
> *Then, like remeeting an old friend,*
> *Eagerly greet the clear light of death.*
> —THE SEVENTH DALAI LAMA,
> "Advice to an Abbot"

BREAKING THE CYCLE:
THE PATH OF LIBERATION

An ancient Tibetan teaching maintains that "meditation on death will, at the beginning, turn one's mind toward the Dharma; in the middle it will spur one on; and in the end, because of it, one will realize death as the Absolute Nature." Death in the Tibetan tradition awakens us to a realm beyond cyclic existence that, far from being a nihilistic void, is the basis of all existence. Similarly, in the path of inner Tantra, sexual yogas simulating the stages of dissolution at the moment of death lead to realization of the subtlest levels of consciousness and the birth of nondual, enlightened awareness.

In Tibet, Tantric Buddhism merged with indigenous shamanistic and Bon traditions, resulting in powerful methods through which enlightenment could be achieved within a single lifetime. Recognizing the luminous continuum of the enlightened mind in the midst of the ongoing cycles of birth and dissolution, the Hevajra Tantra states, "By the very forces whereby others are ensnared, the Tantric gains supreme liberation." Far from advocating exclusions, the path of Tantra takes all phenomena into its embrace. As an early master explained, "Cling to the sacred and disdain the profane and you will be sunk in the ocean of life and death forever." Once the judgmental attitudes stemming from identification with the self are dropped, phenomena are revealed in their intrinsic purity—the co-emergence of emptiness and appearance. "Since practitioners of Tantra realize all phenomena as inherently pure," wrote Longchenpa, the fourteenth-century meditation master, "they can transform everything into a means of liberation."

The methods of the Tantric path were preserved in Tibet's monasteries but were practiced with equal effectiveness by yogins and yoginis free of institutional encumbrances or support. Committed to direct experience of the awakened state, Tantric initiates rely predominantly on the oral precepts—the Whispered Lineage—referred to metaphorically as the "Dakini's Breath" in honor of the mystical partners in the yogin's quest for enlightenment. Practicing in caves and other secluded places, Tantric yogins and yoginis meditate on the psychic channels, inner winds, and subtle essences within the body that, once controlled, give rise to the Innate Mind of Clear Light. The practices of the inner Tantra not only prepare the adept to recognize death as an opportunity for supreme awakening but, more essentially, to bring forth our inherent Buddha-Nature, revealing in this very lifetime the numinous ground of reality itself.

In the meditative practice of *tummo*, the fire of the inner wisdom-dakini at the base of the central channel melts the seminal essences stored at the crown of the head and unites the body's male and female energies at the heart chakra. The resultant bliss—inseparable from all-pervading Emptiness—enables the practitioner to dissociate from mundane consciousness and reach successively deeper levels of meditative absorption. Relying on the male and female polarities within one's own body, the practice of tummo transmutes the energy of passion into enlightened awareness, giving birth to our intrinsic Buddha-Nature. As the Seventh Dalai Lama described:

> *The dakas and dakinis dance blissfully*
> *In the psychic veins and secret drops.*
> *Mundane perception is severed from consciousness*
> *And all emanations become radiantly pure.*
> *Through the unification of male and female essences*
> *Bliss and emptiness arise as one.*

Although some schools of Tibetan Buddhism believe enlightenment can be achieved by relying solely on one's inner wisdom-consort, many lamas claim otherwise. "At a certain point in the mastery of the completion stage," says Lama Yeshe, "a consort is necessary for bringing all the pervading energy winds into the central channel . . . opening the heart center completely and experiencing the profoundest level of clear light."

For ordinary beings the Innate Mind of Clear Light manifests not only at the time of death but also at the moment of sexual climax. Because of habitual obscurations, however, most of us fail to recognize these luminous openings, and what could be a profound opportunity becomes instead a cause of regret and depletion. But if we can transform the energies of death and sexuality through yogic means, then we can reverse the propensities that lead to rebirth in cyclic existence and attain supreme enlightenment in this very lifetime. The "Essence of All-Beneficial Ambrosia," an eighteenth-century Tibetan treatise, expresses the essential stages of this profound transformation:

Mind fixed on the bliss and mudra of the consort
A rain of innate joy pours down.
As if embracing reality itself,
One melts into the sphere of spontaneous ecstasy.

In Dzogchen—the Great Perfection, regarded as the highest and most esoteric of the Buddha's teachings—passion is neither rejected nor transformed but recognized as radiant awareness. "Look into the intrinsic freshness of your desire," said Yeshe Tsogyal, consort of Padmasambhava, "and there is boundless light."

Without relying on external rites or on the transformation practices of the Tantric yogas, Dzogchen is based on the direct experience of the Nature of Mind, which is described as self-liberated and beyond all limitation. Tibetan Buddhist and Bon traditions both assert that Buddhahood can be achieved naturally by resting in the Primordial Luminescence of Mind Nature, a state of immanent awareness beyond conceptual thought and identical in essence with the Clear Light that manifests at death. Lopon Tenzing Namdak, the supreme head of the Bonpo lineage, explained: "The Natural State is our intrinsic condition. It is unproduced and uncreated and like vast space undergoes neither change nor evolution. Discursive thoughts pass through it like birds pass through the sky, leaving no trace."

Stories abound in Tibet of secret Dzogchen practitioners who while leading ordinary lives were never apart from Rigpa, or primordial awareness. When they died they were so attuned to the subtle essence of their own inner elements that they dissolved into bodies of light, leaving behind only hair and nails. Having transcended death and rebirth, such realized beings can, out of compassion, choose voluntarily to re-enter the realm of cyclic existence. As Tulku Chökyi Nyima, the seventh incarnation of a great eighteenth-century yogin, explains: "For those who possess the confidence of realization, dying and the intermediary realm are like a game, a form of entertainment. But for those whose confidence in the Absolute Nature is not that stable, these same experiences may be terrifying."

Jamyang Khyentse Chökyi Lodrö (1896-1959) and his consort Khandro Tsering Chöden, Derge, eastern Tibet. One of the most outstanding scholars and meditation masters of this century, Khyentse Rinpoche married at the age of sixty at the insistence of his students and benefactors. Within a matter of years his waning health was completely restored, and his hair, which had grown white, returned to its original color. Recognized as a great dakini, his consort Tsering Chöden continues to this day to give teachings and spiritual empowerments.

Mountain sanctuary, Tirdrom, central Tibet. In caves above sacred hot springs, Padmasambhava and his consort-bride, Yeshe Tsogyal, meditated in this secluded valley for seven years. It was in this sacred place toward the end of the eighth century that Yeshe Tsogyal—daughter of the Tibetan king—perfected the inner yogas and attained highest enlightenment. Her energy continues to inspire and suffuse the mind-streams of the nuns and yoginis who live and practice here. Praising Yeshe Tsogyal for her spiritual accomplishments, Padmasambhava declared:

> *O yogini who has mastered the Tantra,*
> *The human body is the basis for*
>   *realizing wisdom.*
> *Although the bodies of men and women*
>   *are equally endowed*
> *If a woman has strong aspiration, her*
>   *potential is higher.*

OPPOSITE
Padmasambhava and Yeshe Tsogyal in Ecstatic Embrace, thangka painting. Seated in *yabyum,* Padmasambhava and Yeshe Tsogyal represent the inseparability of nirvana and samsara—or the union of absolute reality and the fleeting apparitional forms that to the unenlightened are a source of distraction and dissipation. In the path of inner Tantra, desire is used as a force of transformation, burning through the habitual obscurations and states of inner contraction that separate us from the primordial expanse of vision and light.

"Without a consort, a partner of skillful means, there is no way that you can experience the mysteries of Tantra."
—PADMASAMBHAVA TO YESHE TSOGYAL

> *Our nectars merged as a single elixir . . .*
> *Self and other dissolved in radiant*
>   *awareness . . .*
> *Bliss penetrating Emptiness is no other*
>   *than the Great Perfection*
> *Innate joy arising as utter openness.*
> —YESHE TSOGYAL TO PADMASAMBHAVA

On a high cliff in Derge, eastern Tibet, Lama Nima, a Chöd practitioner, blows a thigh-bone trumpet scavenged from the funeral grounds, invoking spirits to dismember his body and sever all notions of self-cherishing. Performed in wild and haunted places, the practice of Chöd liberates the yogin from cyclic existence by vanquishing the fear that stems from identification with the ego and the physical body. By summoning what is most dreaded and openly offering that to which we are most attached, new levels of awareness open within ourselves and others. As Lama Nima says: "Chöd reveals the intrinsic purity of all phenomena and emotions. Just as fear magnifies its objects, so too does fearlessness bring confidence and joy. . . . In Tantra there is nothing to renounce, rather we must relate to all things openly and directly. . . . Striving for enlightenment, we should be like an eagle soaring off a high cliff attached to nothing, leaving nothing behind."

OPPOSITE
Caves used for *muntri,* or dark retreat, Lubrak, northern Nepal. "If we remain in darkness, we will discover the radiance of the Natural State. If we take that as the basis of practice, we will quickly attain Buddhahood. . . . The wisdom eye opens and we will be able to see everything in the three worlds. This is the purpose of dark retreats."
—LOPON TENZING NAMDAK

Chatral Senge Dorje Rinpoche seated on a tiger skin, Yangleshö, Nepal. Considered by many to be the greatest living master of Dzogchen—the highest and most subtle of Tibetan Buddhist teachings—Chatral Rinpoche spent much of his life wandering in wild, uninhabited places. Guiding his close disciples in the practices of the Dzogchen Nyingtik—the innermost essence—Chatral Rinpoche resides much of the year in the "hidden land" of Yolmo Kangri. This excerpt from his "Hymn to Yolmo" evokes the qualities of this mystical sanctuary:

Once preoccupied by disease and death,
  happiness and the pursuit of pleasure,
I now rejoice in this hidden dwelling.
The snowy surface of the upper slopes
glow like the planet Venus.
All around nothing but rocky crags and
  deep forests—defying all direction.
Countless siddhas achieved realization
  here, subsisting on wild roots and mush-
  rooms, flowers, and nettle soup. . . .
Following the path of emptiness and bliss
May you too achieve the Great Perfection!

Togden Amting in his hermitage, Tashi Jong, India. Relying on the Whispered Lineage of oral precepts as transmitted in the Kargyu tradition, Amting embodies the quintessence of the yogic path. Seated in a yogic posture that opens the body's subtle energy channels, he demonstrates *tummo*, the yoga of inner heat. The bliss and nonconceptual awareness generated by the fire of tummo spreads throughout the cells of the body, unveiling the Innate Mind of Clear Light. "Although Dzogchen may point to our essential nature more directly," Amting explains, "unless you have the highest capacity you're apt to miss it altogether. Through the practices of the channels, inner winds, and the body's subtle essences, realization is certain."

Mindroling Trichen Rinpoche and his daughter Khandro Tsering Palden, incarnation of the dakini Karma Orgyen Tsomo, Clementown, India. One of the most highly revered lamas of the Nyingma school of Tibetan Buddhism, Mindroling Trichen is popularly known as "the sleeping yogi." An accomplished master of the yoga of Clear Light, Rinpoche spends most of his time in bed. Acting from a state in which the distinctions between dream and reality have resolved into radiant clarity, Mindroling Trichen is sought for divinations and spiritual guidance. As he explains, "The essence of realization is resting in the Clear Light, visualized as a crimson, open-petalled lotus at the body's heart center. By gaining mastery, day and night, in the practice of natural light, compassion blooms like a flower from within and the chaos of dreams gives way to all-penetrating, luminous awareness."

Kalu Rinpoche (1905-1989), one of the foremost Kagyu masters of this century, standing in front of the Boudhanath Stupa, Kathmandu Valley, Nepal. In 1904 Kalu Rinpoche's future parents were in meditative retreat. One night they dreamed they were visited by the great meditation master and scholar Jamyang Kongtrol, who announced he was coming to stay with them and asked to be given room. Not long after this night Dolkar Chung Chung discovered she was pregnant. "As a mother gives birth to a child, so the mind, once its nature is discovered, gives birth to enlightenment. As surely as we are born from a womb, so surely can we give birth to enlightenment by directly realizing the empty, clear, and unimpeded nature of the mind."

—KALU RINPOCHE (Photograph by Thomas Laird)

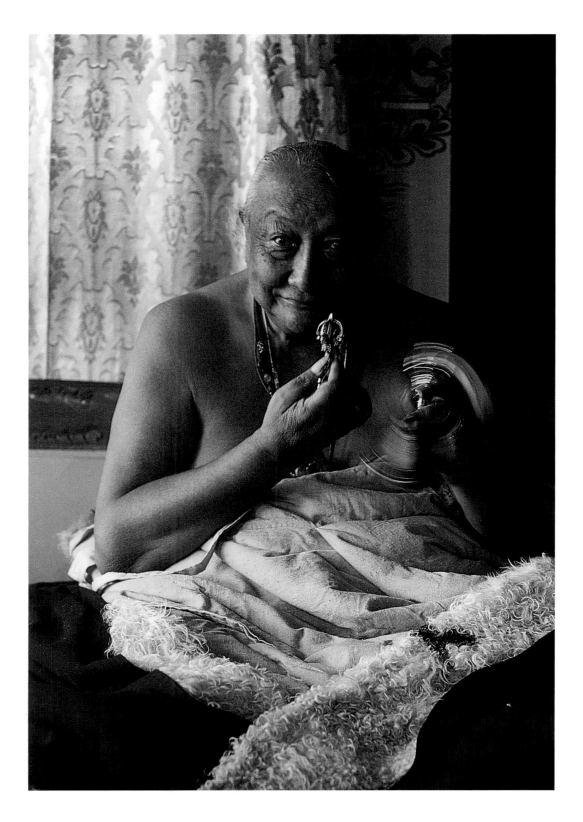

H. H. Dilgo Khyentse Rinpoche (1910-1991), Shechen Tennyi Dargye Ling Monastery, Kathmandu Valley, Nepal. Tutor to the present Dalai Lama and recognized as the mind incarnation of the great Jamyang Khyentse Wangpo, Khyentse Rinpoche was highly revered as one of the greatest exponents of Dzogchen—the teachings of the Great Perfection.

OPPOSITE
Khyentse Rinpoche's *purchang* (cremation palace), Satsam Chorten, below Paro Takstang, Bhutan, November 4, 1992.
"Never forget how swiftly this life will be over, like a flash of summer lightning or the wave of a hand. Now that you have the opportunity to practice Dharma, do not waste a single moment on anything else, but practice with all your energy."
—H. H. Dilgo Khyentse Rinpoche, *The Heart Treasure of the Enlightened Ones*

My delight in death is far, far
  greater than
The delight of traders at making vast
  fortunes at sea,
Or of the lords of the gods who vaunt
  their victory in battle;
Or of those sages who have entered
  the rapture of perfect meditative
  absorption.
So just as a traveler who sets out on
  the road when the time has come to go,
I will remain in this world no longer,
But will dwell in the stronghold of
  the great bliss of deathlessness.
  —LONGCHENPA, FOURTEENTH-
  CENTURY DZOGCHEN MASTER

Senge Tenzing Rinpoche, abbot of the Bonpo monastery Tashi Menri Ling in Dolanji, India, instructing disciples in the practice of powa. "The practice of powa is very important," Senge Tenzing says. "Through a combination of breath control, mantras, and visualization techniques we can learn to transfer our own or others' consciousness at the time of death to the highest Buddha fields. If practiced intensively for one or two weeks a tiny hole appears at the crown of the head into which a grass straw can be inserted as a sign of accomplishment. One should practice diligently until this sign manifests. As the great Marpa said, 'If you study powa, then at the time death approaches you will have no despair. . . . You will be filled with cheerful confidence.'"

OPENING THE SKY DOOR

The great Tibetan meditation master Jigme Lingpa wrote that when we die we should be like a bird soaring in the sky. The sky for Tibetans is synonymous with the celestial realms, the abode of the Buddhas, and the origin of Tibet's lineage of divine kings. As an image of the unobstructed expanse of the liberated mind, the sky is a central metaphor and support for meditation in the most esoteric of Tibetan Buddhist and Bon traditions.

"There are teachings for one to become enlightened," said Marpa, the great translator and father of the Kargyu lineage, "but I have a teaching that offers enlightenment without meditation." In the practice of *powa*, brought to Tibet from India in the eleventh century, the yogin learns to transfer his or someone else's consciousness to the paradise of Amitabha—the realm of infinite light. A method to help those who meet with fatal accidents or oneself as one's own elements are dissolving at the time of death, the highest form of powa involves directly recognizing the Mind Nature at the moment of death and dissolving unobstructedly into Primordial Luminescence. Through powa one bypasses the bardo and avoids rebirth in the six realms of cyclic existence. As an ancient Dzogchen text proclaims, "The ocean of birth and death evaporates as its cause, ignorance of the nature of mind, dissolves."

At Drigung Monastery in central Tibet, a family from Lhasa arrives, carrying the body of their deceased father in a wooden box. In the early morning the boards are pried open and the corpse— swathed in white prayer scarves—is seated in the monastery's central courtyard. Following the practices contained in an eighth-century text entitled "Opening the Door of the Sky," the monks sit before the body and perform powa, transferring the consciousness of the dead man directly to the celestial spheres. The rite continues until the top of the skull begins to swell, indicating that the consciousness has been successfully ejected from the body. The corpse is then carried on the back of one of the monks up the steep slope behind the monastery.

Stuffed animals and human heads hang from the rafters of a Bon temple dedicated to pre-Buddhist protector deities in Tangma, Tibet. Proximity to death, Tibetans believe, deepens our awareness of the subtler levels of mind and grounds us more firmly in reality.

Preparing a corpse for a sky funeral, Tibet, late nineteenth century.

All great beings of the past have died;
Buddhas and Bodhisattvas, saints and kings alike.
The righteous as well as the sinful,
All must one day face death.
How can you be any different?
—LAMA GUNTANG KONCHOK DRONME,
"Conversations with an old Man"

At the top of the ridge, on a platform of stones encircled by prayer flags, the *tomden,* or yogin-butcher, unwraps the body and slices it from head to toe, exposing the underlying flesh and bones. Drawn by the smoke from the juniper fire and the smell of fresh meat, huge vultures begin to gather on the surrounding rocks. The dead man's friends and family add handfuls of purifying juniper needles to the smoldering incense burner; the fragrant smoke rises as an ephemeral link between the human world and the world of unseen spirits. His soul already transferred to celestial space, the dead man's body is used to benefit other living beings—those who offer as well as those who consume. The majestic vultures—thought by Tibetans to be manifestations of flesh-eating dakinis—glide down from the high ridges and surrounding rocks and dance restlessly around the tomden and the unveiled corpse.

"Shey, shey" (eat, eat), shouts the tomden, stepping back off the stone platform with his flaying knife. The birds descend, enveloping the dead man's body in a frenzy of dark, shifting wings. The man next to me—a friend of the deceased—turns and says: "In Tibet we are told we should witness a sky funeral at least once. Seeing what awaits all of us, we won't waste our lives."

Like a Bodhisattva shaman the tomden goes back in amid the vultures and begins to dismember the skeleton, throwing arm and leg bones to the ravenous birds. Then, with a stone mallet he pulverizes the remaining bones—the first parts of the body to form are thus freed of their constraining shapes. Reciting mantras he takes the skull and crushes it with a large rock. He mixes the brain and powdered bones with tsampa flour and again invites the birds to feast. Soon there is nothing left; only the wisps of smoke from the juniper fire drifting across the bare stones. The birds of appetite fly heavily to the crest of the ridge to digest, then slowly, one by one or in pairs, they soar off into the heavens—black shapes fading against a pale, unending sky.

As dogs and crows pick at whatever morsels remain at the site of offerings, several children sit with the tomden laughing and drinking tea. As I watch I reflect that the charnel grounds are a place not so much of endings as of new beginnings, of lives deepened and renewed. For only in confronting death, as Tibetans maintain, can we truly begin to celebrate life—the struggle for security replaced by a vaster vision of fearlessness and unabating openness.

Offering ourselves unequivocally in death and in love we overcome the delusions of self-clinging that keep us spinning on the wheel of life. Free of the gravity of entrenched attachments and fixed beliefs we soar unencumbered in the cloudless sky of our intrinsic nature, reuniting with what the Bonpos call the "Great Mother of Infinite Space"—the source of all creativity and manifestation, of all birth and death.

> *Nothing at all is born*
> *Nothing at all will die*
> *There is nothing that is bound*
> *There is nothing liberated.*
> —THE MAHASIDDHA SAVARIPA

Seated before a corpse swathed in offering scarves, the powa master of Dringungtil Monastery, central Tibet, ejects the consciousness of the dead person beyond the bardo and the six realms of cyclic existence to the Buddha fields of Infinite Light. "In essence, powa means to prevent our awareness—which is wisdom inseparable from emptiness—from falling into further confusion. . . . The consciousness totally merges with the nature of infinite space."
—TULKU ORGYEN

This mind of yours is emptiness and
  luminosity inseparably conjoined.
Without birth or death, it is the Buddha
  of Immortal Light. . . .
When you recognize the pristine nature of
  your mind as no other than the Buddha
Looking into your own mind is resting
  in the mind of the Buddha.

—BARDO THÖDOL
  (Tibetan Book of the Dead)

Monks carry the corpse to the site of offerings. "Our bodies are what we are most attached to," says one of the monks. "That's why offering one's body carries the greatest merit." Tibetans believe that one should benefit other beings at every stage of one's life. After completion of the powa ceremony, the corpse is traditionally offered to the great vultures and lammergeiers that frequent the charnel grounds.

Vultures descend on the flayed corpse. "Offering bodies to the birds is the same as reciting mantras. It brings merit and benefit to the dead person as well as to the family and friends who bring him here. While cutting up the corpse I try to keep a pure and compassionate mind. How would you feel if someone felt repulsed cutting up your body?"

—TOMDENLA

The tomden retrieves the skeleton after the birds have picked it free. Tibetans say that everyone should witness a sky funeral at least once. It brings home the transience and impermanence of life, urging us not to waste the precious opportunity afforded by a human life. "When one realizes that life is the expression of death and death is the expression of life, that continuity cannot exist without discontinuity, then there is no longer any need to cling to one and fear the other."
—CHÖGYAM TRUNGPA RINPOCHE

A Vision of the Charnel Grounds, detail from a seventeenth-century thangka painting. The charnel grounds embody the Tantric injuncture to transform all experience, however horrifying, into enlightened awareness. The ecstatic skeleton holding in his upraised hand a skull cup brimming with spiritual ambrosia reminds the yogin of the impermanence and intrinsic selflessness of all phenomena. Change is the very essence of life, our resistance to it the source of all sorrow and disappointment.

BIBLIOGRAPHY

Allione, Tsultrim. *Women of Wisdom.* Boston and London: Routledge and
    Kegan Paul, 1984.

Andrugtsang, Gompo Tashi. *Four Rivers, Six Ranges: A True Account of
    Khampa Resistance to the Chinese in Tibet.* Dharamsala: Library of
    Tibetan Works and Archives, 1973.

Aris, Michael. *Hidden Treasures and Secret Lives.* Delhi: Motilal Benarsidass,
    1988.

Avedon, John. *In Exile from the Land of Snows.* London: Michael Joseph, 1984.

Aziz, Barbara, and Matthew Kapstein. *Soundings in Tibetan Civilization.* New
    Delhi: Manohar Publications, 1985.

Batchelor, Stephen. *The Tibet Guide.* London: Wisdom Publications, 1987.

Bell, Sir Charles. *The People of Tibet.* Oxford: Clarendon Press, 1928.

———. *The Religion of Tibet.* Oxford: Clarendon Press, 1931

Beyer, Stephen. *The Cult of Tara: Magic and Ritual in Tibet.* Berkeley and Los
    Angeles: University of California Press, 1973.

Campbell, Joseph. "Tibet: The Buddha and the New Happiness." In *The Masks
    of God: Oriental Mythology.* New York: Viking Penguin, 1962.

Chang, Garma C. C. *The Hundred Thousand Songs of Milarepa.* Boulder, Colo.,
    and London: Shambala Publications, 1977.

Chokyi Lodro, Jamyang Khyentse. "Heart Advice." Translated from the Tibetan
    by Sogyal Rinpoche, Rigpa Fellowship, 1981.

Chöpel, Gedun. *Tibetan Arts of Love.* Introduced and translated by Jeffrey
    Hopkins. Ithaca, N.Y.: Snow Lion Publications, 1992.

Chophel, Norbu. *Folk Culture of Tibet.* Dharamsala: Library of Tibetan Works
    and Archives, 1984.

Crystal Cave: A Compendium of Teachings by Masters of the Practice Lineage.
    Edited by Ward Brisick. Translated from the Tibetan by Erik Pema
    Kunsang. Hong Kong and Kathmandu: Rangjung Yeshe Publications,
    1990.

Dharmarakshita. *The Wheel of Sharp Weapons.* Translated from the Tibetan by
    Geshe Ngawang Dhargyey, Sharpa Tulku, Khamlung Tulku, Alexander
    Berzin, and Jonathan Landaw. Dharamsala: Library of Tibetan Works
    and Archives, 1976.

Dhondrup, K. *Songs of the Sixth Dalai Lama.* Dharamsala: Library of Tibetan
    Works and Archives, 1981.

———. *The Water Bird and Other Years: A History of the Thirteenth Dalai
    Lama and After.* New Delhi, 1986.

Dowman, Keith. *Masters of Mahamudra: Songs and Histories of the Eighty-
    Four Buddhist Siddhas.* Albany: State University of New York Press,
    1985.

———. *The Power Places of Central Tibet: A Pilgrim's Guide.* London:
    Routledge and Kegan Paul, 1988.

———. *Sky Dancer: The Secret Life and Songs of the Lady Yeshe Tsogyal.*
    London: Routledge and Kegan Paul, 1984.

Dudjom Rinpoche, Jikdrel Yeshe Dorje. "The Alchemy of Realization."
    Translated from the Tibetan by John Myrdhin Reynolds. Kathmandu:
    Simhananda Publications, 1978.

———. "Heart-Essence of the Great Masters." Translated from the Tibetan by
    Bhakha Tulku Pema Tenzing and Constance Wilkinson. Kathmandu,
    1989.

———. *The Nyingmapa School of Tibetan Buddhism: Its Fundamentals and
    History.* Edited and translated by Gyurme Dorje and Matthew Kapstein.
    Boston: Wisdom Publications, 1991.

———. "A Prayer to Recognize My Own Faults and Keep in Mind the Objects
    of Refuge." Translated from the Tibetan by Bhakha Tulku Pema Tenzing
    and Constance Wilkinson. Kathmandu, 1989.

Elchert, Carole, ed. *White Lotus: An Introduction to Tibetan Culture.* Ithaca,
    N.Y.: Snow Lion Publications, 1990.

Forbes, Ann Armbrecht. *Settlements of Hope: An Account of Tibetan Refugees in
    Nepal.* Cambridge, Mass.: Cultural Survival, 1989.

Ford, Robert. *Wind between the Worlds.* New York: David McKay, 1987.

Goderchen, Terton Rigdzin. *The Aspiration of Kuntuzangpo.* Translated from
    the Tibetan by Keith Dowman. Kathmandu: Diamond Sow
    Publications, 1981.

Goldstein, Melvyn C. "Lhasa Street Songs: Political and Social Satire in
    Traditional Tibet." *Tibet Journal* 7, nos. 1-2 (1982): 56-66.

———. *A Modern History of Tibet,* 1913-1951: The Demise of the Lamaist
    State. London: Oxford University Press, 1989.

Guenther, Herbert V. *The Life and Teachings of Naropa.* London: Oxford
    University Press, 1963.

———. *The Royal Song of Saraha: A Study in the History of Buddhist Thought.*
    Seattle: University of Washington Press, 1969.

———. *The Tantric View of Life.* Berkeley and London: Shambala, 1972.

Gyaltsen, Khenpo Konchog. *In Search of the Stainless Ambrosia.* Ithaca, N.Y.:
    Snow Lion Publications, 1988.

Gyatso, Geshe Kelsang. *Clear Light of Bliss: Mahamudra in Vajrayana
    Buddhism.* London: Wisdom Publications, 1982.

Gyatso, Tenzin, H. H. the Fourteenth Dalai Lama. *The Bodhgaya Interviews.*
    Edited by José Ignacio Cabezon. Ithaca, N.Y.: Snow Lion Publications,
    1988.

———. "Compassion and the Individual." Dharamsala, India.

———. *Freedom in Exile: The Autobiography of the Dalai Lama of Tibet.* Edited by John Curtis. London: Hodder and Stoughton, 1990.

———. "The Global Community and the Need for Universal Responsibility." Dharamsala, India.

———. *Kindness, Clarity, and Insight.* Ithaca, N.Y.: Snow Lion Publications, 1984.

———. *A Policy of Kindness.* Edited by Sidney Piburn. Ithaca, N.Y.: Snow Lion Publications, 1990.

———. *Universal Responsibility and the Good Heart.* New York: Potala Publications, 1985.

Gyatso, Tenzin, and Jeffrey Hopkins. *Kalachakra Tantra: Rite of Initiation.* Boston: Wisdom Publications, 1985.

Gyurme Dorjee, Minling Terchen. *The Jewel Ladder: A Preliminary Nyingma Lamrim.* Dharamsala: Library of Tibetan Works and Archives, 1990.

Hicks, Roger. *Hidden Tibet: The Land and Its People.* London: Element Books, 1988.

Kalu Rinpoche. *The Dharma that Illuminates All Beings Impartially like the Light of the Sun and the Moon.* Albany: State University of New York Press, 1986.

Karmay, Sampten Gyaltsen. *The Great Perfection.* Leiden, Holland: E. J. Brill, 1988.

Kelly, Petra, Gert Bastian, and Pat Aiello. *The Anguish of Tibet.* Berkeley: Paralax Press, 1991.

Khamtrul Rinpoche. "Nectar for Snow-Covered Ears." Translated from the Tibetan by Hubert Decleer. Kathmandu, 1989.

Khangkar, Dr. Lobsang Dolma. *Lectures on Tibetan Medicine.* Edited by K. Dhondup. Dharamsala: Library of Tibetan Works and Archives, 1986.

Khyentse, Dilgo. "Heart Treasure of the Enlightened Ones." Essence of Buddhism. New Delhi: Tibet House, 1986.

Kunga, Lama, and Brian Cutillo. *Drinking the Mountain Stream.* New York: Lotsawa, 1978.

Lati Rinpoche and Jeffrey Hopkins. *Death, Intermediate State and Rebirth in Tibetan Buddhism.* London: Ryder, 1979.

Lauf, D. I. *Secret Doctrines of the Tibetan Book of the Dead.* Boulder, Colo.: Shambala Publications, 1977.

Lhalungpa, Lobsang P. *The Life of Milarepa.* Boston and London: Shambala, 1984.

Lingpa, Rigdzin Jigme. *The Dzogchen Innermost Essence Preliminary Practice.* Edited by Brian Beresford. Translated from the Tibetan by Tulku Thondrup. Delhi and Dharamsala: Library of Tibetan Works and Archives, 1982.

———. "The Seal of Wisdom Essence: The Most Secret Way to Accomplish the Lama from the Heart Essence of the Vast Expanse." Translated from the Tibetan by David Christiansen, Kathmandu, 1987.

———. "A Wonderous Ocean of Advice for the Practice of Retreatants in Solitude." Translated from the Tibetan by David Christiansen. London, 1987.

Lodo, Lama. *The Bardo Teachings: The Way of Death and Rebirth.* Ithaca, N.Y.: Snow Lion Publications, 1987.

Majupuria, Indra. *Tibetan Women.* Lashkar, India: M. Devi, 1990.

Manjusrimitra. *Primordial Experience: An Introduction to Dzogchen Meditation.* Translated from the Tibetan by Namkhai Norbu and Kennard Lipman. Boston and London: Shambala Publications, 1986.

Mipham, Lama. "The Torch Which Dispells Darkness." Translated by Konchog Tendzin. Kathmandu, 1989.

Mullin, Glenn H. *Death and Dying in the Tibetan Tradition.* Chicago: Penguin, 1987.

———. "A Long Look Homeward: An Interview with the Dalai Lama of Tibet." New York: Potala Publications, 1987.

———. *Path of the Bodhisattva Warrior: The Life and Teachings of the Thirteenth Dalai Lama.* Ithaca, N.Y.: Snow Lion Publications, 1988.

———. *Selected Works of the Dalai Lama VII.* Ithaca, N.Y.: Snow Lion Publications, 1982.

Norbu, Dawa. *Red Star Over Tibet.* New York and London: Collins, 1974.

Norbu, Jamyang. *Warriors of Tibet: The Story of Aten and the Khampas' Fight for the Freedom of Their Country.* London: Wisdom Publications, 1986.

Norbu, Namkhai. *The Cycle of Day and Night.* Edited by John M. Reynolds. Berkeley: Zhang Zhung Editions, 1984.

———. *The Mirror: Advice on Presence and Awareness.* Arcidosso, Italy: Shang-Shung Editions, 1983.

———. *The Mirror of the Luminous Mind.* Rome, 1983.

Norbu, Thinley. *Gypsy Gossip.* Kathmandu, 1980.

———. *Magic Dance: The Display of the Self Nature of the Five Wisdom Dakinis.* Paris: Sedag, 1981.

———. *White Sail.* Boston and London: Shambala Publications, 1992.

Norbu, Thubten Jigme, and Colin Turnbull. *Tibet: Its History, Religion and People.* New York: Simon and Schuster, 1968.

Nuden Dorje, Taksham. "The Mystic Songs of Yeshe Tsogyal." Translated from the Tibetan by Keith Dowman. Kathmandu: Diamond Sow Publications, 1980.

Nyima, Chokyi. *The Bardo Guidebook.* Hong Kong and Kathmandu: Rangjung Yeshe Publications, 1991.

———. *Jewel of the Heart: Mahamudra Teachings on the Nature of the Mind.* Translated from the Tibetan by Erik Pema Kunsang. Kathmandu: Rangjung Yeshe Publications, 1987.

———. *The Union of Mahamudra and Dzogchen.* Edited by Marcia B. Schmidt. Translated from the Tibetan by Erik Pema Kunsang. Hong Kong and Kathmandu: Rangjung Yeshe Publications, 1986.

Nyingpo, Namkhai. *Mother of Knowledge: The Enlightenment of Yeshe Tsogyal.* Translated from the Tibetan by Tarthang Tulku. Berkeley: Dharma Publishing, 1983.

Padmasambhava. "Clear Light: A Guide to the Hidden Land of Pemako." Discovered by Rinchen Riwoche Jedong Pung. Translated from the Tibetan by Bhakha Tulku Pema Tenzing, 1989.

———. Dakini Teachings: Padmasambhava's Oral Instructions to Lady Tsogyal. Translated from the Tibetan by Erik Pema Kunsang Boston: Shambala, 1990.

———. "Relieving the Heart's Darkness: Guidebook to the Hidden Land of Pemako." Discovered by Dorje Thogme. Translated from the Tibetan by Bhakha Tulku Pema Tenzing, 1989.

Pal, Pratapaditya. Art of Tibet. Berkeley and London: University of California Press and Los Angeles County Museum of Art, 1983.

Paltrul Rinpoche. The Practice of the Essence of the Sublime Heart Jewel, View, Meditation and Action: The Propitious Speech from the Beginning, Middle and End. Translated from the Tibetan by Thinley Norbu Rinpoche. New York: Jewel Publishing House, 1984.

Phalu, Khache. Khache Phalu's Advice on the Art of Living. Translated from the Tibetan by Dawa Norbu. Dharamsala: Library of Tibetan Works and Archives, 1987.

Piburn, Sidney, ed. The Nobel Peace Prize and the Dalai Lama. Ithaca, N.Y.: Snow Lion Publications, 1990.

Rangdrol, Tsele Natsok. The Lamp of Mahamudra. Translated from the Tibetan by Erik Pema Kunsang. Boston and London: Shambala, 1989.

———. The Mirror of Mindfulness. Translated from the Tibetan by Erik Pema Kunsang. Kathmandu: Rangjung Yeshe Publications, 1987.

Reynolds, John Myrdhin. "Yungdrung Bon: The Eternal Tradition." Freehold, N.J., 1991.

Richardson, Hugh E. Adventures of a Tibetan Fighting Monk. Singapore: White Lotus Publications, 1986.

———. Tibet and Its History. London: Oxford University Press, 1962.

Sakya, Jamyang, and Julie Emery. Princess in the Land of the Snows. Boston: Shambala, 1990.

Sangpo, Khetsun. Tantric Practice in Nyingmapa. Translated and edited by Jeffrey Hopkins. Ithaca, N.Y.: Gabriel/Snow Lion Publications, 1982.

Shabkar, Lama, Jatang Tsogdruk Rangdrol. Flight of the Garuda. Translated from the Tibetan by Erik Pema Kunsang. Hong Kong and Kathmandu: Rangjung Yeshe Publications, 1986.

Shantideva. A Guide to the Bodhisattva's Way of Life. Translated from the Tibetan by Stephen Batchelor. Dharamsala: Library of Tibetan Works and Archives, 1979.

Snellgrove, David L. The Nine Ways of Bon. London: Oxford University Press, 1967.

Snellgrove, David L., and Hugh E. Richardson. A Cultural History of Tibet. Boulder, Colo.: Prajna Press, 1968.

Sogyal Rinpoche. Dzogchen and Padmasambhava. Berkeley: Rigpa Fellowship, 1989.

———. The Tibetan Book of Living and Dying. San Francisco: HarperCollins, 1992.

Sopa, Geshe Lhundub, Roger Jackson, and John Newman. The Wheel of Time: The Kalachakra in Context. Ithaca, N.Y.: Snow Lion Publications, 1985.

Stein, R. A. Tibetan Civilization. London: Faber and Faber, 1972.

Stevens, John. Lust for Enlightenment. Boston and London: Shambala, 1990.

Tendzin Namdak, Lopon. Bonpo Dzogchen Teachings. Transcribed and edited by John Myrdhin Reynolds. Amsterdam, 1992.

Thogme, Ngulchu. "The Thirty-Seven Bodhisattva Precepts." Translated from the Tibetan by Bhakha Tulku Pema Tenzing and Pat Roddy, 1990.

Thondrup, Tulku. Buddha Mind: An Anthology of Longchen Rabjam's Writings on Dzogpa Chenpo. Edited by Harold Talbott. Ithaca, N.Y.: Snow Lion Publications, 1989.

———. Buddhist Civilization in Tibet. New York and London: Routledge and Kegan Paul, 1987.

Thurman, Robert A. F., and Marilyn M. Rhie. Wisdom and Compassion: The Sacred Art of Tibet. New York: Harry N. Abrams, 1991.

Trungpa, Chogyam. Born in Tibet. London: George Allen and Unwin, 1966.

———. Crazy Wisdom. Boston and London: Shambala, 1991.

———. Cutting through Spiritual Materialism. Berkeley: Shambala Publications, 1973.

———. The Heart of the Buddha. Boston and London: Shambala, 1991.

———. Journey without Goal: The Tantric Wisdom of the Buddha. Boulder and London: Prajna Press, 1981.

———. The Myth of Freedom. Berkeley and London: Shambala, 1976.

———. Shambala: The Sacred Path of the Warrior. Boulder and London: Shambala, 1984.

Trungpa, Chogyam, and Francesca Freemantle. The Tibetan Book of the Dead: The Great Liberation through Hearing in the Bardo. Berkeley and London: Shambala, 1975.

Tsogyal, Yeshe. The Life and Liberation of Padmasambhava. Berkeley: Dharma Publishing, 1978.

Tucci, Giuseppe. The Religions of Tibet. London and Boston: Routledge and Kegan Paul, 1980.

———. Tibet: Land of Snows. New York: Stein and Day, 1967.

Tulku, Chagdud. "Life in Relation to Death." Cottage Grove, Oreg.: Padma Publishing, 1987.

Tulku, Tara. "A New Dwelling: An Interview with Tara Tulku." Parabola 9, no. 3 (1984): 30-39.

Urgyen, Tulku. Vajra Heart. Kathmandu: Rangjung Yeshe Publications, 1988.

Von Furer-Haimendorf, Christoph. The Renaissance of Tibetan Civilization. Delhi: Oxford University Press, 1990.

Willis, Janice D., ed. Feminine Ground: Essays on Women and Tibet. Ithaca, N.Y.: Snow Lion Publications, 1989.

Yeshe, Lama Thubten. Introduction to Tantra: A Vision of Totality. Boston and London: Wisdom Publications, 1987.

———. "Life, Death, and after Death." Boston and London: Wisdom Publications, 1983.

INDEX

PHOTOGRAPHY CREDITS

All photographs courtesy of Thomas L. Kelly, with the exception of the following: